Potato Salad

Potato Salad

Fifty Favorite Recipes

Barbara Lauterbach

Photographs by Reed Davis

CHRONICLE BOOKS

SAN FRANCISCO

Library of Congress Cataloging-in-Publication Data:

Lauterbach, Barbara.
    Potato salad : fifty favorite recipes / by Barbara Lauterbach.
    108 p.   22.3 x 20.4 cm.
    Includes index.
    ISBN 0-8118-3337-2 (pbk.)
    Cookery (Potatoes) 2. Salads. I. Title.
    TX803.P8 L38 2002
    641.6'521—dc21
            2001028814

Printed in China

Prop and food styling by Alison Attenborough, Yolanda Yorke,
and Ronnda Hamilton

Designed by Madeleine Corson Design, San Francisco

Distributed in Canada by Raincoast Books
9050 Shaughnessy Street
Vancouver, BC V6P 6E5

10 9 8 7 6 5 4 3 2 1

Chronicle Books LLC
85 Second Street
San Francisco, California 94105
www.chroniclebooks.com

Lentil and Potato Salad (page 102) reprinted from *Happy Cooking!*, by Jacques Pépin,
©1994 by Jacques Pépin. Used by permission of KQED Books & Tapes.

Potato Salad Marcella (page 101) reprinted from *Essentials of Italian Cooking*,
by Marcella Hazan, ©1992 by Marcella Hazan. Used by permission of
Alfred A. Knopf, a division of Random House, Inc.

Potato Salad, Florentine Style (page 100) reprinted from *The Fine Art of
Italian Cooking*, by Giuliano Bugialli, ©1977 by Giuliano Bugialli. Used by
permission of Times Books, a division of Random House, Inc.

Potato Salad with Tomatillo Sauce (page 98) reprinted from *The Savory Way*,
by Deborah Madison, ©1990 by Deborah Madison. Used by permission
of Bantam Books, a division of Random House, Inc.

Hot Potato and Bratwurst Salad (page 87) reprinted from *The German
Cookbook*, by Mimi Sheraton, ©1965 Mimi Sheraton. Used by
permission of Random House, Inc.

Sweet Potato and Smoked Turkey Salad (page 48) reprinted from *Cooking Smart*
by Sharon Tyler Herbst. Used by permission of the author.

Miracle Whip® Salad Dressing and Salad Spread is a registered trademark of Kraft
General Foods, Inc. Hellmann's® Mayonnaise is a registered trademark of CPC
International, Inc. Tabasco® Pepper Sauce is a registered trademark of the McIlhenny
Company. Velveeta® Cheese is a registered trademark of Kraft Foods, Inc.

FOR LORA BRODY

WHO PROVIDED ME THE COURAGE TO START,
THE ENCOURAGEMENT TO FINISH

A MENTOR AND, ABOVE ALL, A FRIEND

CONTENTS

Introduction — 9

The Basics

My Favorite Potatoes for Salad — 12

Eyes and Nays of Potatoes — 13

Master Recipes for Cooking Potatoes — 16

Toasting Nuts — 17

Mayonnaise — 19

**The All-Americans:
Salads from Around the Country**

Recipes from Family and Friends

Blue-Ribbon Southern Potato Salad — 22

Marsh Family Mashed Potato Salad — 23

New England Spring Potato Salad — 24

Camp Island Potato Salad — 25

New England Mustard-Pickle Potato Salad — 26

Roasted Garlic Potato Salad — 27

Rosemary-Orange Potato Salad — 29

Red Pesto Potato Salad — 30

Tailgate Potato Salad — 34

New Year's Day Good Luck Salad — 35

Moulton Farm Potato Salad — 37

Chef Woolley's Grilled Potato Salad — 38

The Frog Potato Salad — 40

Horseradish Potato Salad — 42

Potato Salad for a Crowd — 43

Meat and Poultry Salads

Home-Run Potato Salad — 44

Steak and Potatoes Salad — 45

Tarragon Lamb Potato Salad — 47

Sweet Potato and Smoked Turkey Salad — 48

New Hampshire Mapled Ham and Potato Salad — 50

Seafood Salads

Smoked Oyster Potato Salad — 51

Fabulous Fourth Salmon and Potato Salad — 53

Lobster Roll Potato Salad — 54

Smoked Trout and Potato Salad — 56

Crabmeat and Potato Salad — 57

Sunday Morning Smoked Salmon Potato Salad — 58

The Internationals:
Salads from Around the World

Some Like It Hot:
Potato Salad "Casseroles"

Potato Salad Molly Malone   63

Jo's Asian Potato Salad   64

Alpine Potato and Cheese Salad   66

An Irish Potato Salad   67

Greek Potato Salad   69

Pesto Potato Salad   70

"Stop and Go" Italian Potato Salad   72

Marie's French Potato Salad   73

Niçoise Potato Salad   75

Portuguese Potato Salad   76

Curried Potato Salad   78

Russian Potato Salad   79

Potatoes Night Out   83

Pass the Potatoes   85

Hot Potato and Bratwurst Salad   87

Dee Dee's Pennsylvania Dutch Hot Potato Salad   88

Nuremberg Potato Salad   90

Gammy's Hot Potato Salad   91

"No Pressure" French Potato Salad   92

Jansson's Temptation   94

Church Supper Potluck Hot Ham and Potato Salad   95

The Celebrities:
A Collection of My Favorites

Deborah Madison—Potato Salad with Tomatillo Sauce   98

Giuliano Bugialli—Potato Salad, Florentine Style   100

Marcella Hazan—Potato Salad Marcella   101

Jacques Pépin—Lentil and Potato Salad   102

Acknowledgments   105

Index   106

Table of Equivalents   108

As American as apple pie, as homey as a handmade quilt—who doesn't like potato salad? It's a staple at family dinners, picnics, barbecues, country fairs, and church suppers. Clans pass down their recipes from generation to generation and threaten warfare over such issues as peeled or unpeeled, with or without mayonnaise, and with or without pickles.

Woe unto the new bride who would add fresh herbs or use Miracle Whip instead of Hellman's Mayonnaise to dress the heirloom recipe. Southerners hotly defend their potato salad, maintaining that it must include sweet pickle and hard-boiled egg to be authentic, while across the country in California, lemongrass and cilantro are just as often part of the mix. Some like it hot, some like it cold, and some wouldn't consider eating it except at room temperature.

While many Americans think this ubiquitous side dish was invented here, Germans have been enjoying a scoop of *Kartoffelsalat* with their knockwurst and lager as long as the French have been eating their *salade aux pommes de terre* with *jambon*.

Pasta salad has had its day. Now it's time to lift the lowly potato to its rightful place at the center of the table. Thanks to the proliferation of heirloom varieties, as well as Yukon Golds, Red Blisses, and fingerlings no bigger than truffles, potatoes have been elevated to gourmet-food status. Additional good news is that potato salad is inexpensive to make and usually can be whipped up using on-hand ingredients.

Here in New Hampshire, and throughout New England, we consume prodigious amounts of potato salad every summer and numerous hot potato dishes during our long winters. On a beautiful Fourth of July morning, while sitting on my front porch overlooking Lake Winnipesaukee, cookbook author and good friend Lora Brody suggested I write a potato salad cookbook. And this book was born.

In the following pages, you will find both American recipes and international ones. There are New Age salads, fusion versions, and some downright funky creations, too.

In some cases, I've taken the liberty of interpreting potato salad loosely. For example, it has been traditionally regarded as a cold side dish, but thanks to increasing vegetarianism and greater attention to the food pyramid, the potato salad is moving toward the main-dish category. It also turns up hot more often than in the past, sometimes under the guise of a casserole.

Basic potato-cooking techniques appear in the beginning of the book, keeping the subsequent recipes wonderfully short. Many of the salads can be prepared in less than thirty minutes and in some cases can be scaled to feed as few as two or as many as fifty.

In my many years as a cooking teacher and innkeeper, I have seen and continue to see the need and demand for recipes that taste and look good, that can be prepared quickly and economically, and that appeal to both the novice and the experienced cook. This collection of potato salad recipes has been designed to fit that bill.

THE BASICS

Dozens of potato varieties exist, many of them found in only certain parts of the country, and the list grows every year. Low-starch potatoes are best suited for salad making because the slices remain firm. A high-starch potato, such as a russet, will be more absorbent and will fall apart more readily when boiled, while a waxier low-starch potato, such as a Red Bliss, absorbs less water when boiled and holds up to the rigors of being mixed with other ingredients.

The starch of a potato is determined by its variety. If you are in doubt as to the starch content of a particular variety, noted food lecturer and author Shirley Corriher suggests a simple test in her book *Cookwise*: In a large bowl, make a brine solution of 1 cup salt and 11 cups water. Drop the potato in question into the solution. If it floats, it has a low starch content.

With this information at hand, here's how to match the characteristics of various potatoes to achieve the best possible result in a salad that combines potatoes with other ingredients and a dressing.

Potatoes can be classified according to age, texture, taste, color, and variety.

AGE All potatoes start life as "new" potatoes. Some can be kept for months after harvesting without softening or sprouting. Others have a much shorter storage life. This is strictly a function of the variety. A so-called new potato does not change in terms of texture and taste as it ages; it simply deteriorates faster than another variety. For example, a Red Bliss is not a good keeper. Thus, one typically finds it offered as a new potato.

TEXTURE The texture of a potato is mostly a function of its starch content. What is important in terms of potato salad is that potatoes described as waxy tend to hold their shape when cut into cubes, whereas those described as mealy tend to fall apart when cubed.

TASTE If a potato has been properly stored and properly prepared, it will taste good.

COLOR This is mostly an aesthetic value, with buttery types usually having flesh that is more yellow than white.

VARIETY The following potato varieties are the most readily available and are recommended for potato salad. (Crops in different areas of the country will mature at different rates. It's a good idea to know what is produced locally and when it is harvested.) The same potato variety is sometimes known by different names.

Fingerlings Low starch, small (about 1 inch in diameter and 1 to 3 inches long), irregular exterior bumps, pale brown skin (red skin is found in some areas), and waxy yellow flesh; retains shape well. Generally available in late summer and into the fall.

Red Bliss Low starch, small, round, smooth red skin, waxy surface when cut; retains shape well. Available fresh in spring and fall.

White Eastern (sometimes called all-purpose white) Medium starch, round, light brown skin, moist surface when cut; retains shape well. Available fresh in fall, from storage other times of the year. May be used whenever all-purpose potatoes are called for in the recipes.

White Rose (sometimes called Long White) Low starch, long and oval, pale yellow skin, moist surface when cut; retains shape well. Available fresh year-round in California and western states. May be used whenever all-purpose potatoes are called for in the recipes.

Yukon Gold Medium starch, round, pale yellow skin, buttery yellow flesh; retains shape well. Available fresh midsummer in many states, from storage other times of the year.

Other suitable potato varieties that may be available regionally include:

La Rouge and La Soda Low starch, small-sized, round, red skin, white flesh. Grown primarily in Florida, available in the Southeast.

Red Norland and Red Pontiac (sometimes called all-purpose red) Medium to low starch, medium-sized, round to oblong, red skin, white flesh. Grown in the Midwest and Florida. May be used whenever all-purpose potatoes are called for in the recipes.

Superior and Kennebec Medium starch, medium- to large-sized, round, light brown skin, white flesh. Grown in the eastern United States. May be used whenever all-purpose potatoes are called for in the recipes.

In conclusion, potato salads work best with low- or medium-starch potatoes whose waxy texture allows them to hold together when diced and mixed. If the potato variety called for in a recipe is not available, substitute a comparable regional variety.

Things Every Potato Salad Cook Should Know

◎ It is preferable not to peel potatoes before cooking for salad.

◎ The unpeeled potato will retain its shape better while it is being cooked, and it will not become soggy. Also, more nutrients are retained by cooking potatoes with their skins on.

◎ The recipes in this book specify whether or not to peel the potatoes after cooking. Some find the skins aesthetically unappealing, others may enjoy the texture and color contrast of them. If you have a strong preference one way or the other, follow your taste, the salad will still be delicious.

◎ To prepare the potatoes up to 24 hours before making potato salad, cook them according to the preferred method for the recipe and drain in a colander. Remove the potatoes from the colander and halve or quarter them, depending on their size. Peel or not according to the recipe. Return the potatoes to the colander; pour 1 cup of distilled white vinegar over them, shaking gently, which will prevent discoloration of the cooked potatoes. Place the drained potatoes in a bowl, cover with plastic wrap, and refrigerate for up to 24 hours. Proceed with the salad recipe. (If the recipe calls for sprinkling the hot potatoes with vinegar after cooking, eliminate this step.)

◎ Many potato salad recipes call for chopped onion. Some people do not like to eat raw onion, no matter how finely chopped. A delicate onion flavor can be obtained in a potato salad by putting 2 medium, peeled yellow onions, halved, in the cooking water with the potatoes. Remove and discard the onions when the potatoes are done, and proceed with the recipe.

⊚ If you peel potatoes before cooking, soak them in a bowl of cold water to cover until ready to use to prevent discoloration.

⊚ Kosher salt is my salt of preference for use in most cooking, although you may certainly use regular granulated table salt in these recipes. Kosher salt is formed from surface evaporation. It is flaky and dissolves and blends faster than regular granular salt.

⊚ Freshly ground pepper, black or white, is best for salads.

Purchasing Potatoes
⊚ Buy what you'll use within 10 days to 2 weeks.

⊚ Don't buy potatoes with green spots, blemishes, or sprouted "eyes." If they are exposed to light in storage, or stored at too high or too low a temperature, they develop a greenish cast, the result of an increase in the level of toxic alkaloids. The toxins are removed by cooking, but the potatoes will have a bitter taste. The sprouted eyes, the product of age, should be cut out.

⊚ Select potatoes of the same size, so they cook uniformly. If the potatoes are very large, cut them into same-sized pieces before cooking.

Average Number of Potatoes in Two Pounds
Baby: 18 to 20 potatoes
Small: 10 to 14 potatoes
Medium: 6 to 8 potatoes
Large: 2 to 3 potatoes

Storing Potatoes
⊚ Do not wash potatoes before storing, as any remaining moisture clinging to the skins hastens decay. Remove them from plastic bags to avoid trapped moisture, and store in a well-ventilated vegetable bin.

⊚ If not using within 2 weeks, store in a dark, dry, cool place (ideal temperature is 45° to 50°) for up to 3 months. Before using, cut out any eyes or sprouts that have formed.

⊚ Do not refrigerate potatoes, as this turns some of their starches to sugars.

⊚ Do not freeze potatoes, or they will become watery.

Boiling or steaming is the best way to cook potatoes for salad. Other methods may be used, depending on the recipe. Also, cooking potatoes unpeeled results in better flavor and a higher retention of nutrients. Unless otherwise specified, peel the potatoes after cooking for recipes in this book. Allow them to cool just until they can be handled; then, while still warm, dress them according to the recipe. This produces a much more flavorful salad.

Boiling Potatoes

Boiling is ideal for the low-starch waxy potatoes most often used for salad. The timing depends on the number of potatoes and their size.

In a heavy saucepan that accommodates the potatoes without crowding, place the potatoes, water to cover, and about 1 teaspoon salt per quart of water. Cover partially, bring to a boil, and cook until tender when pierced, 20 to 25 minutes after the water has returned to a boil for 2- to 3-inch potatoes.

Avoid piercing the potatoes repeatedly to test for doneness, or too much moisture will seep in and produce a soggy interior. Use a knife for probing, as a fork permits more water to reach the center. When done, drain the potatoes in a colander and return them to the warm cooking pan briefly, tossing them over low heat to dry them. Proceed with the salad recipe.

Steaming Potatoes

Steaming is an excellent way to retain the texture of the potato and works particularly well for medium-starch potatoes. It also reduces the loss of nutrients. Steam new potatoes or small potatoes whole in their skins. Peel larger potatoes, cut into pieces, and then steam.

Select a pan with a steamer-basket insert or a pan large enough to accommodate a steamer basket. Add water to the pan to reach just below the basket. Bring the water to a boil and add the potatoes to the basket. They should fit in a single layer. If you have more than one layer, steam the potatoes in batches or boil them. If the potatoes are very large, cut them in half and steam them cut-side down.

Cover the pan and steam until done, checking to make sure the water does not boil away. Small potatoes ($1\frac{1}{2}$ inches in diameter) will take up to 15 minutes; larger potatoes will take 18 to 20 minutes, depending on the number of potatoes and their size.

When done, transfer the potatoes to a colander to drain. Remove the basket and pour the water out of the pan. Return the potatoes to the warm pan and toss over low heat to dry them. Proceed with the salad recipe.

Although the nuts called for in most of the recipes in this book can be used as they come from the can or the bag, toasting them lends richness and develops their crunchiness. Unless the recipe specifies whole nuts, chop them before toasting, as the cut sides of the nuts allow the oils to come to the surface, resulting in more flavor.

You may toast them in a skillet on the stove top, or on a baking sheet in the oven. You may also microwave them, but I find this method tedious, as they must be turned every 30 to 40 seconds.

To toast nuts in a skillet: This works best for a small quantity, $\frac{1}{2}$ cup or less. Warm the skillet over medium heat, add the nuts, and stir frequently until you begin to see a slight browning and the nuts are fragrant. This should take 2 to 3 minutes. Take them off the heat and immediately transfer to a small bowl or plate, as they will continue to brown if left in the skillet.

To toast nuts in the oven: Preheat the oven to 350°F. Spread the nuts on a baking sheet and place in the oven. Toast until they begin to brown and are aromatic, 6 to 8 minutes, checking them after 3 or 4 minutes and stirring them at that time. Remove from the oven and pour the nuts onto a plate or into a bowl.

Whichever method you use, watch the nuts carefully, as their high fat content causes them to go quickly from perfectly toasted to burned.

Making mayonnaise from scratch is not difficult to master, and it is a skill worth having in your culinary repertoire. Some cooks prefer not to use raw eggs, however. They fear the presence of salmonella bacteria, despite the fact that contamination is very rare. If you are concerned, any good-quality commercial mayonnaise can be used in place of homemade in the recipes in this book. I have not found the mayonnaise recipes calling for partially cooked eggs very good or worth the trouble.

The type of oil you use in the mayonnaise depends on the salad to be dressed. You may also add more than one kind, such as I cup vegetable oil and ½ cup olive oil, or a combination of vegetable and peanut oils. The robustness of the oil will depend on the salad. A salad composed of strong flavors can take a dressing made with a large proportion of heavier oil, such as a full-bodied olive oil or walnut oil.

I large whole egg, plus I large egg yolk
I½ teaspoons Dijon mustard
I tablespoon fresh lemon juice or white wine vinegar
Salt and freshly ground pepper to taste
I½ cups vegetable oil

To make in a food processor or blender: Place the whole egg, egg yolk, mustard, lemon juice or vinegar, salt, and pepper in a food processor. Process for 20 seconds to "melt" the salt and thicken the egg. With the motor running, add the oil as slowly as you can at first, just a dribble, increasing the flow as you see the mixture becoming creamy. When all of the oil has been added, taste and adjust the seasoning. If the sauce is too thick, add a drop or two of water and process to mix.

To make by hand: Follow the directions for the machine method, using a bowl and whisk. Anchor the bowl to the work surface by placing a damp dish towel beneath it.

Should the mayonnaise curdle, all is not lost. Simply turn the mixture into a large (4-cup) measuring pitcher. Add an additional ½ teaspoon mustard to a clean bowl. Stir the curdled mixture, then, I tablespoon at a time; whisk it vigorously into the bowl with the mustard. (You may instead use a handheld mixer for this.) Keep adding the curdled mayonnaise, I tablespoon at a time, mixing well after each addition. You should have a nice, stiff mayonnaise at the end. Be sure to go slowly at first so that the emulsion, or thickening, starts.

THE ALL-AMERICANS: SALAD

FROM AROUND THE COUNTRY

Blue-Ribbon Southern Potato Salad

THIS SALAD, AKA MAMA'S POTATO SALAD, WON A BLUE RIBBON FOR ANNA LEAK IN THE MOUNT OLIVE PICKLE COMPANY'S POTATO SALAD CONTEST, HELD EVERY OCTOBER DURING THE DIXIE CLASSIC FAIR IN WINSTON-SALEM, NORTH CAROLINA. ONE OF THE CONTEST RULES REQUIRES THAT THE SALADS CONTAIN EITHER MOUNT OLIVE DILL OR SWEET PICKLE CUBES. LEAK, A HAIRDRESSER IN WINSTON-SALEM, CHANGED HER GRANDMOTHER'S RECIPE ONLY BY ADDING PIMIENTOS AND MAYONNAISE. THE RECIPE FIRST APPEARED IN THE *WINSTON-SALEM JOURNAL* OF OCTOBER 6, 1999, IN AN ARTICLE ON THE CONTEST, AND IT WAS SENT TO ME BY EMILY AND EVAN RICHEY, OF WINSTON-SALEM.

SERVES 6 TO 8

8 red or brown all-purpose potatoes, peeled and cut into ½-inch cubes

½ cup diced celery

½ cup diced green bell pepper

¼ cup diced yellow onion

3 hard-boiled eggs, chopped

1 jar (8 ounces) sweet pickle cubes or 1 cup diced sweet pickle

1 small jar (4 ounces) pimientos, drained, dried on paper towels, and diced

DRESSING

1 cup mayonnaise, homemade (page 19) or high-quality purchased

½ cup sour cream

1½ teaspoons yellow mustard

Dash of sugar

Dash of salt

Cook the potatoes according to the Master Recipe (page 16) for steaming potatoes, testing for doneness after 8 minutes. Continue to cook, if necessary, until done but not overly soft. Drain and let cool.

In a large bowl, mix together the cooled potatoes, celery, green bell pepper, onion, eggs, pickle cubes, and pimientos.

To make the dressing, in a separate bowl, mix together the mayonnaise, sour cream, mustard, sugar, and salt. Add to the potato mixture, toss gently but thoroughly, cover, and chill before serving.

Marsh Family Mashed Potato Salad

MY DAUGHTER, LISA, IS A GRADUATE STUDENT AT HARVARD UNIVERSITY. SHE FIRST TASTED THIS RECIPE DURING A SESSION OF THE PFORZHEIMER HOUSE COOKING CLUB, WHICH MEETS ONCE A MONTH AS A WELCOME DIVERSION FROM THE STRAINS OF ACADEMIC LIFE. HER FELLOW STUDENT ERICA MARSH GOT IT FROM HER MOTHER, MARY E. MARSH, OF RICHMOND, VIRGINIA. LISA, WHO HAD NEVER TASTED ANYTHING LIKE IT, THOUGHT IT SHOULD BE INCLUDED IN THIS COLLECTION. THE CONSISTENCY, WHICH RECALLS THE SMASHED POTATOES ONE ENCOUNTERS IN TRENDY RESTAURANTS, IS UNLIKE ANY POTATO SALAD WE YANKEES HAVE EVER ENCOUNTERED. ERICA SAYS THAT THIS IS POTATO SALAD TO HER, AND UNTIL SHE WENT NORTH TO COLLEGE, SHE HAD NEVER HAD A CHUNKY POTATO SALAD. ONLY MIRACLE WHIP WILL WORK HERE.

SERVES 6

1½ pounds red all-purpose potatoes
1 to 1½ cups Miracle Whip
   Salad Dressing
½ cup finely chopped sweet onion
   such as Vidalia or Maui
½ cup sweet pickle relish
2 hard-boiled eggs, chopped
1 tablespoon sugar
Salt and freshly ground pepper to taste

Cook the potatoes according to the Master Recipe (page 16) for boiling potatoes. When cool enough to handle, peel, cut into ½-inch cubes, and place in a large bowl.

Mash the warm potatoes with a potato masher or a large spoon. Add 1 cup of the Miracle Whip and keep mashing the potatoes until they resemble hot mashed potatoes. There will be some lumps. Add the onion, pickle relish, eggs, sugar, salt, and pepper and keep mashing. Add up to ½ cup more Miracle Whip if needed to achieve the consistency of rich, creamy mashed potatoes with little bits of pickle, egg, onion, and potato for texture. Taste and adjust the seasoning.

Don't be surprised by the amount of Miracle Whip you may end up using. Place the salad in a serving bowl, cover, and refrigerate up to overnight. It may be served chilled or at room temperature.

New England Spring Potato Salad

SPRING IS SLOW IN COMING TO NORTHERN NEW ENGLAND, BUT ALONG ABOUT THE BEGINNING OF MAY, AFTER THE FORSYTHIA AND BEFORE THE LILACS, WHISPERS OF "FIDDLEHEADS ARE UP" ARE HEARD AROUND LOCAL COMMUNITIES. WHETHER YOU HAVE A SECRET HARVEST SPOT FOR THE DELICATE FRONDS OR YOU PURCHASE THEM AT THE LOCAL SUPERMARKET, FIDDLE-HEADS LIFT YOUR SPIRITS LIKE NO OTHER SPRING TONIC. NAMED BECAUSE OF THEIR RESEMBLANCE TO A VIOLIN, THEY HAVE A FLAVOR SOMEWHERE BETWEEN AN ASPARAGUS AND AN ARTICHOKE, AND THE TIME-CONSUMING PREPARATION THEY REQUIRE IS WORTH THE EFFORT. TRY THEM SIMPLY STEAMED, WITH BUTTER AND LEMON, IN SOUP, STIR-FRIES, OR THIS SALAD.

SERVES 6

2 pounds Yukon Gold potatoes
2 tablespoons white wine vinegar
1/3 cup chopped red onion
1/2 pound fiddlehead ferns

DRESSING

3 tablespoons fresh lemon juice
Salt and freshly ground pepper to taste
6 tablespoons extra-virgin olive oil

Cook the potatoes according to the Master Recipe (page 16) for steaming potatoes. When cool enough to handle, peel the potatoes and cut them into 1/2-inch chunks. Place in a large bowl and sprinkle with the vinegar and the onion while still warm. Set aside to cool.

To prepare the fiddleheads, soak them in a sink filled with cold water for 5 minutes. Remove the brown papery coating from each frond, discarding it, and trim any ragged stalk ends. Pour water to a depth of 1 inch into a steamer pan or saucepan and bring to a boil. Put the fiddleheads on a steamer rack or basket, place the rack or basket in the pan, cover, and cook for 5 minutes. Remove the steamer rack or basket and place the fiddleheads under cold running water to set the color. Drain well and pat dry.

To make the dressing, in a small bowl whisk together the lemon juice, salt, and pepper. Then whisk in the olive oil until emulsified.

Just before serving, combine the fiddle-heads, potatoes, and dressing. Toss gently to mix, then serve. Do not add the dressing to the salad more than 30 minutes in advance of serving. The acid of the lemon will leach out the color of the fiddleheads, rendering them an unappetizing khaki.

NOTE Once you have cleaned the fiddle-heads, you can blanch them in boiling water for 1 minute, drain, run them under cold water, drain again, pat them dry, and freeze tightly wrapped for up to 1 month. Then, when ready to make the salad, steam as directed without thawing.

Camp Island Potato Salad

WHEN MY FRIENDS LIZ LAPHAM AND HER HUSBAND, BEV, EXTEND A "DINNER CRUISE" INVITATION, NO ONE REFUSES! I HAVE BEEN FORTUNATE ENOUGH TO JOIN THEM ON SEVERAL SUMMER EVENINGS FOR A LOVELY EXCURSION ON LAKE WINNIPESAUKEE. WE SET SAIL FROM THE MEREDITH TOWN DOCK AND HEAD FOR CAMP ISLAND, ONE OF THE MANY SMALL ISLANDS THAT DOT THE LAKE. WE TIE UP, THEN A TABLE IS UNFOLDED AND SET UP ON THE DOCK, COMPLETE TO THE CANDLES. BEV FIRES UP THE GRILL FOR HIS FAMOUS STEAKS, CORN IS COOKED IN A POT OVER A PROPANE BURNER, AND LIZ PRODUCES THIS WONDERFULLY CRUNCHY SALAD. THE SUN DIPS INTO THE LAKE, THE STARS APPEAR, AND ALL'S RIGHT WITH THE WORLD. THE SALAD TRAVELS WELL ON LAND AS WELL AS SEA.

SERVES 6 TO 8

1 pound red new potatoes

1 package (10 ounces) frozen petite peas, thawed and drained

1 cup cauliflower, chopped small

1 cup celery, chopped small

1 cup cashew nuts, chopped small

1/4 cup chopped scallions, white part only

1/4 cup chopped red onion

Lettuce leaves

Chopped chives for garnish

DRESSING

1/2 cup sour cream

1 cup high-quality purchased Ranch-style salad dressing

1/2 teaspoon garlic salt

1 teaspoon salt

1/2 teaspoon freshly ground pepper

Cook the potatoes according to the Master Recipe (page 16) for boiling potatoes. When cool enough to handle, peel and cut into 1/4 inch cubes. Place in a large bowl and add the peas, cauliflower, celery, cashews, scallions and red onion. Toss gently to mix.

To make the dressing, in a small bowl, mix together the sour cream, ranch dressing, garlic salt, salt, and pepper. Pour the dressing over the vegetable mixture and toss gently but thoroughly. Cover with plastic wrap and refrigerate for 4 hours or up to 24 hours. When ready to serve, pile on a platter lined with lettuce leaves and garnish with the chopped chives.

New England Mustard-Pickle Potato Salad

FOR A TRADITIONAL CLAMBAKE, THE MENU TYPICALLY FEATURES STEAMED CLAMS, LOBSTERS, CORN ON THE COB, AND STEAMED OR BAKED POTATOES. IN PLACE OF THE LAST I LIKE TO SERVE THIS POTATO SALAD. THE PIQUANT FLAVOR OF THE MUSTARD-PICKLE DRESSING PLAYS WELL WITH THE SWEET AND SALTY SEAFOOD.

SERVES 6 TO 8

2½ pounds Red Bliss or
   red new potatoes
½ cup diced yellow onion
½ cup diced celery
Salt and freshly ground pepper to taste
1 whole mustard pickle (optional)

DRESSING
½ cup mayonnaise, homemade (page 19)
   or high-quality purchased
½ cup chopped mustard pickle,
   homemade or purchased (see note)
1 tablespoon (or less) cider vinegar

Cook the potatoes according to Master Recipe (page 16) for boiling potatoes. When cool enough to handle, cut into ½-inch-thick slices and place in a large bowl. Add the diced onion and celery and toss gently. Season with salt and pepper.

To make the dressing, in a small bowl, mix together the mayonnaise and chopped mustard pickle. If the mixture is very thick, add up to 1 tablespoon vinegar in 1-teaspoon increments; you may not need the full 1 tablespoon.

Pour the dressing over the potato-onion-celery mixture and toss gently. Cover and refrigerate for at least 1 hour or overnight to allow the flavors to blend.

Serve the salad directly from refrigerator. If you like, garnish the top of the salad with the whole pickle, slicing it lengthwise but not cutting all the way through and fanning out the slices.

NOTE There are several brands of mustard pickle on the market, although many New Englanders make their own in cucumber season. Good recipes can be found in two well-known volumes, *Fannie Farmer Boston Cooking-School Cookbook* and *Joy of Cooking*.

Roasted Garlic Potato Salad

THIS IS A GARLIC LOVER'S DELIGHT! ROASTED GARLIC IS POPULAR, AND ITS SWEET, BUTTERY FLAVOR, MELLOWED BY ROASTING, ADAPTS WELL TO POTATOES. THE USE OF ALL-PURPOSE OR YUKON GOLD POTATOES WILL GIVE YOU "SOFTER" SLICES THAN MANY OTHER TYPES.

SERVES 6 TO 8

2 pounds Yukon Gold or brown
　all-purpose potatoes
2 tablespoons white wine vinegar
$1/3$ cup finely chopped red onion
$1/3$ cup finely chopped flat-leaf or
　curly parsley

DRESSING

2 to 3 tablespoons roasted garlic (see note)
$1/2$ cup mayonnaise, homemade (page 19)
　or high-quality purchased
Salt and freshly ground pepper to taste

Cook the potatoes according to the Master Recipe (page 16) for boiling potatoes. When cool enough to handle, peel and cut into $1/4$-inch-thick slices. Place the slices in a large bowl and sprinkle with the vinegar while still warm. Let the potatoes cool to room temperature and add the red onion and parsley.

Meanwhile, prepare the roasted garlic for the dressing and set aside.

To make the dressing, in a small bowl, stir together the roasted garlic and the mayonnaise. Season with salt and pepper.

Pour the mayonnaise mixture over the potatoes and mix gently but thoroughly. Serve immediately, or cover and refrigerate for up to 24 hours, then serve chilled.

NOTE To roast garlic, do not peel or separate the cloves. Cut a thin slice off the top of each head, exposing the cloves, then remove the paperlike white skin from the garlic heads. Wrap each head separately in aluminum foil. Bake the heads in a preheated 350°F oven until soft to the touch, about 1 hour. Let cool for 10 minutes. Separate the cloves and squeeze each clove from the root end to extract the pulp from the papery sheaths. The pulp may be stored in an airtight container in the refrigerator for several days. One average garlic head yields a scant 3 tablespoons of pulp.

Rosemary-Orange Potato Salad

FRESH ROSEMARY MAKES THE BIG DIFFERENCE IN THIS SALAD. ALTHOUGH THE GROWING SEASON FOR THE FRAGRANT HERB IS SHORT IN NEW HAMPSHIRE, I BRING A POT INDOORS AT THE FIRST FROST AND ENJOY ITS PUNGENT AROMA—AND THIS SALAD—ALL WINTER LONG. SERVE THE SALAD AS A DELICIOUS ACCOMPANIMENT TO GRILLED FISH OR ROAST PORK.

SERVES 6 TO 8

DRESSING

1 cup mayonnaise, homemade (page 19)
   or high-quality purchased
1 1/2 teaspoons thawed orange
   juice concentrate
1 1/2 teaspoons grated orange zest
1 1/2 teaspoons chopped fresh rosemary
2 tablespoons heavy cream
2 tablespoons fresh orange juice

2 pounds red or brown all-purpose potatoes
2 tablespoons white wine vinegar
Salt and freshly ground pepper to taste
Fresh rosemary sprigs for garnish

To make the dressing, in a bowl, combine all the dressing ingredients, mix well, and let stand for 1 hour to allow the flavors to blend, or cover and refrigerate for up to 4 days.

Meanwhile, cook the potatoes according to the Master Recipe (page 16) for boiling potatoes. When cool enough to handle, peel, cut into 1/4-inch cubes, and place in a large bowl. Sprinkle with the vinegar, season with salt and pepper, and let cool to room temperature.

Add the dressing to the cooled potatoes and toss to mix thoroughly. Cover and refrigerate until chilled. Serve chilled, garnished with rosemary sprigs.

Red Pesto Potato Salad

WHEN THE EXQUISITE, BUT ALL TOO SHORT, NEW HAMPSHIRE SUMMER APPROACHES ITS END, MOULTON'S FARM STAND, WHICH IS NEAR MY HOME, OVERFLOWS WITH AN EMBARRASS-MENT OF RICHES, NOT THE LEAST OF WHICH ARE THE TOMATOES. FROM THE GIANT GLOBES OF BRANDYWINE HEIRLOOMS TO THE TAUT-SKINNED RED ROMAS, THE VARIETY IS OVERWHELMING. THE SWEET TASTE OF THE EARTH ONE EXPERIENCES WHEN EATING A VINE-RIPENED TOMATO CANNOT BE BETTERED, BUT A PROPERLY DRIED ROMA IS AS ADDICTIVE AS A POTATO CHIP! TRY THIS SALAD IF YOU HAVE A GOOD SUPPLY OF SUN- OR OVEN-DRIED TOMATOES.

SERVES 6 TO 8

RED PESTO

1 cup dried roma (plum) tomatoes, either home-dried (see note) or purchased

1 cup boiling water, if using purchased tomatoes

½ cup fresh basil leaves, thoroughly dried

1 bunch fresh flat-leaf parsley, thoroughly dried and roughly chopped

½ cup extra-virgin olive oil, or more if needed

2 cloves garlic, minced

½ cup pine nuts

½ cup freshly grated Parmesan cheese

Salt to taste

2 pounds red new potatoes

2 tablespoons white wine vinegar

1 cup artichoke hearts, either marinated and drained or frozen, thawed, and cooked according to package directions, halved

Salt and freshly ground pepper to taste

First, make the pesto. If you are using store-bought dry-packed tomatoes, rehydrate them by placing them in a bowl, adding the boiling water, letting them stand for 10 to 15 minutes, and then draining. If you are using store-bought oil-packed tomatoes, drain them and add the oil to the measuring cup to make up part of the ½ cup oil.

Place the tomatoes, basil leaves, and parsley in a food processor fitted with the metal blade. With the motor running, slowly add the oil through the feed tube, and then add the garlic. Stop the motor, remove the lid, and add the pine nuts. Replace the lid and pulse 1 or 2 times until the nuts are chopped and the pesto is creamy, adding more oil if necessary.

Turn the pesto into a bowl and stir in the cheese. Taste for seasoning, adding salt if needed. (Parmesan is salty, so be careful.) You should have about 1 cup. You may store the pesto for up to a month in the refrigerator in a covered container. Top it with a thin film of olive oil before capping.

Cook the potatoes according to the Master Recipe (page 16) for boiling potatoes. When cool enough to handle, peel if desired, then cut into cubes measuring no more than ¼ inch. Place the cubes in a bowl, add the vinegar and toss gently. Add the artichoke hearts, pesto, salt, and pepper and toss gently again.

(Recipe continues on page 32.)

(Red Pesto Potato Salad continued)

Cover and refrigerate for up to 24 hours if not serving immediately. Bring to room temperature before serving.

NOTE I've tried "sun"-drying tomatoes by the traditional method, but let's face it: New Hampshire isn't Naples, even in the summer. I ended up with flies and spoiled tomatoes. This method for drying tomatoes works for me, but be careful or you'll eat half of them before you get them in the fridge!

Have ready as many roma (plum) tomatoes as you want to dry (I usually do them in 2- to 3-pound batches), vegetable oil spray, olive oil, and kosher salt. Preheat the oven to 375°F.

While the oven is preheating, split the tomatoes in half lengthwise, then squeeze them slightly over the sink or a bowl to release excess juice and some seeds. Line one or more baking sheets with aluminum foil and spray with vegetable oil spray. Place the tomatoes, cut-side up, on the foil, and drizzle lightly with olive oil. Sprinkle lightly with kosher salt.

Place the baking sheet(s) in the oven and reduce the temperature to 200°F. Bake, checking the tomatoes every hour until they are shriveled and dried. The timing will depend on the ripeness of the tomatoes. It usually takes from 4 to 6 hours. Remove from the oven and place the tomatoes on a drying rack to cool. Store in the refrigerator, covered, or freeze in plastic bags. They will keep in the refrigerator for up to 3 weeks and in the freezer for several months.

Tailgate Potato Salad

THE FIRST NIPPY NIGHTS IN OCTOBER HERALD THE MOST GLORIOUS OF NEW HAMPSHIRE'S SEASONS. THE FOLIAGE EXPLODES, AND THOUGHTS TURN TO "CLEANING UP" THE GARDEN AND TIGHTENING UP FOR WINTER. APPETITES PICK UP, AND HEARTY TAILGATE PICNICS ARE POPULAR. WHETHER THEY'RE ROOTING FOR THE LOCAL TEAM, OR TRAVELING OVER TO HANOVER TO WATCH THE BIG GREEN AT DARTMOUTH, NEW HAMPSHIRE FOLKS LIKE A GOOD TAILGATE. ⊙ THIS POTATO SALAD IS DELICIOUS, ESPECIALLY IF THE GRILL IS BROUGHT ALONG AND FAT, JUICY SAUSAGES OR BURGERS ARE SERVED AS AN ACCOMPANIMENT. THE SALAD TRAVELS WELL WHEN PACKED IN A COOLER.

SERVES 6 TO 8

½ pound small sweet potatoes
  (1 large or 2 small)
1½ pounds Yukon Gold potatoes
½-pound piece butternut squash,
  peeled and cut into ¼-inch cubes
¼ cup chopped fresh curly parsley
¼ cup dried cranberries
¼ cup chopped red onion
¼ cup chopped walnuts, toasted (page 17)

DRESSING
½ cup sugar
1 teaspoon dry mustard
½ teaspoon salt
2 tablespoons grated yellow onion
⅓ cup cider vinegar
1 cup canola oil
1 tablespoon celery seed

Preheat the oven to 400°F. Scrub the sweet potatoes with a stiff brush but do not peel. Prick in several places with the tines of a fork. Bake just until tender when pierced with a fork, about 30 minutes. The timing will depend on the size of the potatoes. Alternatively, scrub and prick the potatoes and microwave on high for 6 to 8 minutes. Don't overcook, or they won't cut nicely. Let cool completely and cut into ¼-inch cubes.

Cook the Yukon Gold potatoes according to the Master Recipe (page 16) for boiling potatoes. When cool enough to handle, peel and cut into ¼-inch cubes.

Cook the butternut squash cubes in boiling water to cover until just tender, about 5 minutes. Drain well.

While the potatoes are cooking, make the dressing: In a bowl, mix together the sugar, dry mustard, and salt. Stir in the onion and 2 tablespoons of the cider vinegar and mix until smooth. Gradually beat in the oil and the remaining vinegar. Add the celery seed last. Blend well. The dressing can be made up to 2 days ahead, covered, and refrigerated.

In a large bowl, gently mix together the Yukon Gold potatoes, sweet potatoes, squash, and parsley. Add the dried cranberries, red onion, and walnuts, then pour the dressing over all. Mix gently but thoroughly. Cover and refrigerate until serving, then bring to room temperature before serving.

New Year's Day Good Luck Salad

IT IS CUSTOMARY IN THE SOUTH TO EAT BLACK-EYED PEAS FOR LUCK EARLY IN THE NEW YEAR. A FRIEND FROM VIRGINIA BROUGHT THIS SALAD TO A NEW HAMPSHIRE NEW YEAR'S POTLUCK, AND EVERYONE IN ATTENDANCE AGREED THAT THE SALAD WAS A CUSTOM THAT COULD CROSS THE MASON-DIXON LINE ANYTIME!

SERVES 8 TO 10

1 pound Yukon Gold potatoes

2 tablespoons cider vinegar

2 cups cooked dried black-eyed peas (see note)

½ cup chopped green bell pepper

½ cup chopped red bell pepper

¾ cup chopped celery

¾ cup chopped red onion

¾ pound turkey kielbasa, diced (1½ cups) and lightly sautéed

¼ cup finely chopped fresh cilantro

Salt and freshly ground pepper to taste

½ cup sliced radishes (optional)

DRESSING

½ cup canola oil

⅓ cup sugar

4 tablespoons sherry vinegar

¾ teaspoon salt

¾ teaspoon freshly ground pepper

1 teaspoon Tabasco or other hot-pepper sauce

Cook the potatoes according to the Master Recipe (page 16) for boiling potatoes. When cool enough to handle, peel and cut into ¼-inch cubes. Place in a large bowl and sprinkle with the cider vinegar while still warm.

To make the dressing, in a small bowl, whisk together the canola oil, sugar, vinegar, salt, pepper, and hot-pepper sauce until well blended.

Add the black-eyed peas, bell peppers, celery, red onion, sausage, and cilantro to the bowl holding the potatoes. Pour the dressing over all, and mix gently but thoroughly. Season with salt and pepper.

Cover and refrigerate for up to 1 day. Serve chilled or at room temperature. Just before serving, garnish with the radish slices, if desired.

NOTE Although you will not need all the black-eyed peas this method yields, it is easiest to cook the whole amount and reserve the leftovers for another use. Rinse 1 pound (about 2¼ cups) dried black-eyed peas in a sieve, picking out any small pieces of gravel that may be present. Place the peas in a saucepan and add water to cover by 2 inches. Bring to a boil, cover, and boil for exactly 2 minutes. Remove from the heat and let stand in the water for 1 hour. Drain the peas and return to the pan. Add cold water to cover by 2 inches, bring to a boil, reduce the heat to a simmer, and cook the peas until just tender, 45 minutes to 1 hour. Drain, reserving the liquid. Measure out 2 cups drained peas for the salad recipe. Refrigerate the remaining peas in a covered container with a little of the cooking water.

Moulton Farm Potato Salad

MOULTON FARM, LOCATED BETWEEN MEREDITH AND MOULTON-BOROUGH, NEW HAMPSHIRE, HAS BEEN IN THE MOULTON FAMILY FOR THREE GENERATIONS. JOHN MOULTON LEFT HIS TEACHING POSITION SEVERAL YEARS AGO TO SUCCEED HIS FATHER IN MANAGING THE FAMILY PROPERTY, WHICH WAS NAMED A NEW HAMPSHIRE FARM OF DISTINCTION IN 1997. THE FARM'S STAND AREA HAS EXPANDED EVERY YEAR AND PROVIDES SOME OF THE BEST-QUALITY PRODUCE TO BE FOUND ANYWHERE. EVEN THE TINIEST BLEMISH ON A TOMATO KEEPS IT OFF THE DISPLAY. THE SPINACH LEAVES ARE CRISP, TINY, AND GREEN, AND THE EGGPLANTS ARE GLOSSY AND FAT. NEW VARIETIES ARE ALWAYS BEING TRIED, WHICH IS WHY FINGERLING POTATOES, CHIOGGIA BEETS, AND HARICOTS VERTS ARE NO LONGER UNKNOWN IN THIS RURAL CORNER OF THE NORTHEAST. AS A HUGE FAN OF GOOD FRESH VEGETABLES, I CONSIDER MYSELF BLESSED TO LIVE ONLY TWO MILES FROM THE FARM. THIS SALAD USES A VARIETY OF BOUNTY FROM THE STAND. YOU MAY SUBSTITUTE YOUR FAVORITE VEGETABLES IN THE SAME QUANTITY.

SERVES 6

DRESSING

2 tablespoons white wine vinegar

1 teaspoon Dijon mustard

1 teaspoon salt

1¼ teaspoons freshly ground pepper

1 tablespoon chopped fresh tarragon, or 1 teaspoon dried tarragon, crumbled

⅓ cup extra-virgin olive oil

1 pound fingerling potatoes

2 tablespoons white wine vinegar

½ cup sliced small zucchini, blanched (see note)

½ cup sliced small yellow (summer) squash, blanched (see note)

1 cup sugar snap peas, blanched if desired (see note)

¼ cup chopped red bell pepper

¼ cup chopped green bell pepper

¼ cup chopped red onion

Chopped fresh chives for garnish (optional)

To make the dressing, in a small bowl, combine the vinegar, mustard, salt, and pepper and whisk until the salt is dissolved. Add the tarragon and gradually whisk in the olive oil to form an emulsion.

Cook the potatoes according to the Master Recipe (page 16) for steaming potatoes. When cool enough to handle, cut into ¼-inch-thick slices. Place in a large bowl and sprinkle with the vinegar while still warm, then let cool to room temperature.

Add the zucchini, yellow squash, sugar snap peas, bell peppers, and onion to the cooled potatoes. Pour the dressing over the mixture, then toss gently but thoroughly. Sprinkle with the chives, if desired. Serve immediately, as the vegetables tend to discolor if refrigerated.

NOTE To blanch the vegetables, fill a large bowl or pan with cold water and some ice cubes. Fill a saucepan three-fourths full with water and bring to a rolling boil. Drop in the vegetables and boil for 1 minute. Drain and immediately immerse the vegetables in the ice water. When cold, drain and pat dry.

Chef Woolley's Grilled Potato Salad

MARY ELLEN AND BRIAN SHIELDS ARE THE OWNERS OF THE MANOR ON GOLDEN POND, AN INN WITH A RESTAURANT IN HOLDERNESS, NEW HAMPSHIRE. THEY ENTICED EXECUTIVE CHEF JEFFREY WOOLLEY TO MOVE NORTH AFTER THEY SAMPLED HIS FOOD IN NORTH CAROLINA, WHERE HE LAST WORKED. A GRADUATE OF THE CULINARY INSTITUTE OF AMERICA, WOOLLEY CREATES ELEGANT AND IMAGINATIVE MENUS AND PRESENTS THEM IN THIS BEAUTIFUL COUNTRY SETTING. HE KINDLY SHARED A SUMMER POTATO SALAD WITH ME. YOU'LL HAVE TO IMAGINE THE GLORIOUS VIEW OF THE LAKE.

SERVES 8

2 red bell peppers, halved, deribbed and seeded

1 yellow bell pepper, halved, deribbed and seeded

2 pounds Red Bliss potatoes, cut into $\frac{1}{2}$-inch-thick slices

$\frac{1}{3}$ cup capers, rinsed

1 cup black olives, preferably Kalamata or Niçoise, pitted

$\frac{1}{2}$ cup chopped fresh flat-leaf or curly parsley

DRESSING

$\frac{1}{4}$ cup extra-virgin olive oil

$\frac{1}{4}$ cup champagne vinegar

$\frac{1}{2}$ cup mayonnaise, homemade (page 19) or high-quality purchased

Salt and freshly ground pepper to taste

Light a charcoal or gas grill. Place the bell peppers on the grill and char, turning as needed, until the surface of the pepper is blackened and blistered. Transfer the peppers to a paper or plastic bag and let stand for about 10 minutes. Remove the peppers from the bag, peel away the charred skins and discard. Place the peppers in a covered bowl and refrigerate until needed.

Place the potatoes on the grill, and grill, turning once, until they are tender to the touch, about 3 to 4 minutes on each side.

While the potatoes are cooling, make the dressing: In a small bowl, whisk together the olive oil, champagne vinegar, and mayonnaise until well mixed. Season with salt and pepper. When the potatoes are cool enough to handle, pour the dressing over the grilled potatoes, cover, and marinate overnight in the refrigerator. (Chef Woolley likes to put the potatoes and dressing in a plastic bag to marinate.)

The next day, cut the roasted peppers into long, narrow strips and place in a bowl. Add the capers, olives, and parsley and mix to combine. Add the pepper-olive mixture to the potatoes and mix gently but thoroughly.

Serve immediately, or cover and refrigerate for up to 6 hours. Then serve chilled. Alternatively, transfer to a baking dish and warm in a preheated 350°F oven until heated through, about 20 minutes, or heat in a microwave on high for 4 to 5 minutes. Serve as a hot side dish.

The Frog Potato Salad

THE DRESSING FOR THIS SALAD IS THE HANDS-DOWN FIRST CHOICE OF MANY CENTER HARBOR RESIDENTS. I TAUGHT IT IN ONE OF MY COOKING CLASSES SEVERAL YEARS AGO, AND IT IS NOW ALWAYS REQUESTED WHEN I BRING FOOD TO THE POLL WORKERS AT ELECTION TIME. RETIRED COLONEL LEWIS HANSON, A ONETIME PILOT OF *AIR FORCE ONE* AND TODAY A TOWN SELECTMAN, SAYS IT IS HIS FAVORITE! THE DRESSING RECIPE COMES FROM THE FROG CATERING COMPANY OF PHILADELPHIA, FORMERLY THE FROG COMMISSARY RESTAURANT. STEVEN POSES, OWNER OF THE COMPANY AND AUTHOR OF THE RECIPE, GRACIOUSLY CONSENTED TO ITS USE IN THIS BOOK. I HAVE COMBINED THE DRESSING WITH OTHER INGREDIENTS TO MAKE A COLORFUL POTATO SALAD. POSES SAYS THE DRESSING IS EQUALLY DELICIOUS AS A DIP FOR CRUDITÉS.

SERVES 6 TO 8

2 pounds Yukon Gold potatoes

2 tablespoons white wine vinegar

1 cup grape tomatoes (smaller than a cherry tomato) or cherry tomatoes, stemmed

2 cups broccoli florets, blanched (see note)

3 or 4 marinated artichoke hearts, drained and quartered

1/3 cup Kalamata olives, pitted and chopped

FROG MUSTARD DRESSING

1/4 cup Dijon mustard

1 tablespoon red wine vinegar

1/8 teaspoon salt

1/2 teaspoon freshly ground pepper

1/2 cup corn oil

Cook the potatoes according to the Master Recipe (page 16) for boiling potatoes. When cool enough to handle, peel and cut into 1/4-inch-thick slices. Place in a large bowl and sprinkle with the vinegar while still warm.

To make the dressing, in a small bowl, whisk together the mustard, vinegar, salt, and pepper. Gradually whisk in the corn oil until an emulsion forms. (The dressing may be made up to 2 days ahead and stored, covered, in the refrigerator.)

Add the tomatoes, broccoli, artichoke hearts, and olives to the potatoes (the potatoes should be at room temperature). Pour 3/4 cup of the dressing over the mixture and toss gently but thoroughly. Add more dressing if the mixture is too dry for your taste. Serve immediately.

If you are not serving the salad right away, do not add the broccoli until serving time, as it will turn an unappealing khaki due to the acidity of the vinegar. The salad may be refrigerated, undressed, for up to 2 hours. After being dressed, it should be served immediately.

NOTE To blanch the broccoli florets, fill a saucepan three-fourths full of water and bring to a rolling boil. Drop in the broccoli and boil for 2 minutes. Drain and immediately place under cold running water to set the color. When cold, drain and pat dry.

Horseradish Potato Salad

FANS OF HORSERADISH WILL LOVE THIS ZESTY SALAD. YOU CAN ALTER THE HEAT LEVEL BY THE TYPE AND AMOUNT OF PREPARED HORSERADISH YOU CHOOSE. THE OPTIONAL ADDITION OF JULIENNED TONGUE OR HAM IS DELICIOUS. THIS SALAD IS ALSO GOOD WITH HAMBURGERS FROM THE GRILL.

SERVES 6

2 pounds Red Bliss or red new potatoes

2 tablespoons white wine vinegar

¼ cup finely chopped red onion

1 cup julienned boiled tongue or ham (optional)

½ cup chopped carrot

½ cup chopped celery

DRESSING

2 to 3 tablespoons bottled horseradish, drained (see note)

⅓ cup mayonnaise, homemade (page 19) or high-quality purchased

⅓ cup sour cream or plain yogurt

1 tablespoon minced fresh chives

1 tablespoon finely chopped fresh flat-leaf or curly parsley

Salt and freshly ground pepper to taste

Cook the potatoes according to the Master Recipe (page 16) for steaming potatoes. When cool enough to handle, peel if desired, then cut into ¼-inch-thick slices. Place the potatoes in a large bowl, sprinkle with vinegar, and let cool to room temperature.

To make the dressing, in a small bowl, stir together the horseradish, mayonnaise, sour cream or yogurt, chives, and parsley. Season with salt and pepper.

Add the onion, tongue or ham (if using), carrot, and celery to the cooled potatoes. Pour the dressing over the potato mixture and mix gently but thoroughly. Cover and refrigerate until chilled or for up to 6 hours. Serve chilled.

NOTE Commercially prepared horseradish comes in different heat levels. Read the labels carefully and purchase according to your preference. Horseradish loses its punch quickly, so it is best to buy a new jar if your current supply is over a few weeks old. I prefer to drain off most of the moisture from the horseradish before mixing it with the mayonnaise.

Potato Salad for a Crowd

IN NEW ENGLAND, POTLUCK CHURCH SUPPERS ARE POPULAR EVENTS. THIS RECIPE CAME TO ME FROM A FELLOW PARISHIONER OF TRINITY CHURCH, MEREDITH, NEW HAMPSHIRE, KNOWN LOCALLY AS THE LITTLE WHITE CHURCH ON THE HILL. SOMETIMES DOUBLING A RECIPE IN DIRECT PROPORTIONS DOESN'T WORK. THIS SALAD CAN BE DOUBLED SUCCESSFULLY TO SERVE FIFTY.

SERVES 25

FRENCH DRESSING

2 tablespoons white or red wine vinegar
Salt to taste
Dash of freshly ground pepper
1 clove garlic, minced
6 tablespoons extra-virgin olive oil

5 pounds red or brown all-purpose potatoes
5 hard-boiled eggs, diced
6 tablespoons chopped red bell pepper
6 tablespoons chopped green bell pepper
3 cups thinly sliced celery
$\frac{1}{2}$ cup chopped red onion
1 cup sliced radishes

MAYONNAISE DRESSING

2 cups mayonnaise, homemade (page 19)
  or high-quality purchased
$\frac{1}{4}$ cup yellow mustard
1$\frac{1}{2}$ teaspoons paprika
1 tablespoon salt
1 teaspoon freshly ground pepper

To make the French dressing, in a small bowl, whisk together the vinegar, salt, pepper, and garlic. Gradually whisk in the olive oil until emulsified. Set aside.

Cook the potatoes according to Master Recipe (page 16) for boiling potatoes. When cool enough to handle, peel and cut into $\frac{1}{2}$-inch cubes. Place in a large bowl, sprinkle with the French dressing while still warm, and toss gently. Let cool to room temperature, then add the eggs, bell peppers, celery, onion, and radishes.

To make the mayonnaise dressing, in a bowl, mix together the mayonnaise, mustard, paprika, salt, and pepper.

Pour the mayonnaise dressing over the potato mixture and mix gently but thoroughly. Cover and refrigerate until well chilled or for up to 6 hours. Serve well chilled.

Home-Run Potato Salad

THIS RECIPE WAS INSPIRED BY MY FRIEND AND MENTOR, LORA BRODY; BY HER LOVE OF THE HOMETOWN TEAM, THE BOSTON RED SOX; AND BY THEIR VENERABLE FIELD, FENWAY PARK. NO STRIKE-OUT HERE!

SERVES 6

2 pounds Yukon Gold potatoes

2 tablespoons beer, plus ½ cup beer
  if heating hot dogs in a saucepan

6 hot dogs, ballpark style

½ cup sauerkraut, drained

¼ cup coarsely chopped yellow onion

DRESSING

2 tablespoons beer

1 tablespoon plus 1 teaspoon
  yellow mustard

6 tablespoons vegetable or canola oil

Salt and freshly ground pepper to taste

Cook the potatoes according to the Master Recipe (page 16) for boiling potatoes. When cool enough to handle, peel and cut into ½-inch slices. Place in a bowl, sprinkle with the 2 tablespoons beer while still warm, and toss gently to mix.

While the potatoes are cooking, cook the hot dogs and sauerkraut. Add water to a steamer pan to reach just below the rack once the rack is added. Bring the water to a simmer. Place the sauerkraut and hot dogs on the steamer rack, and place the rack in the pan. Cover and steam until heated through, about 10 minutes. Alternatively, put the hot dogs and sauerkraut in a saucepan with ½ cup beer, place over medium heat, and warm until heated through, about 6 minutes. Drain the hot dogs and sauerkraut if using a saucepan.

Meanwhile, make the dressing: In a small bowl, whisk together the beer and the mustard, then whisk in the oil. Season with salt and pepper.

Add the onion to the cooled potatoes. Cut the hot dogs into bite-sized pieces and add along with the sauerkraut to the potato-onion mixture. Pour the dressing over the potato–hot dog mixture and stir gently but thoroughly. This salad is best if served immediately, or cover and refrigerate for up to 8 hours. Bring to room temperature before serving.

Steak and Potatoes Salad

DO YOU LOVE STEAK AND POTATOES? THE NEXT TIME YOU FIND YOURSELF WITH ONLY A FEW CHUNKS OF COOKED BEEF LEFT IN THE REFRIGERATOR, NOT ENOUGH FOR A MEAL OR EVEN A DECENT SANDWICH, TRY THIS SALAD. IT'S EQUALLY GOOD WITH ROAST BEEF.

SERVES 6

2 pounds Yukon Gold potatoes

2 tablespoons white wine vinegar

$1/4$ cup chopped red onion

2 tablespoons chopped fresh
    flat-leaf parsley

1 cup (more or less) cubed cooked steak
    ($1/2$-inch cube)

1 tablespoon high-quality steak sauce

$1/3$ cup crumbled Roquefort or
    other blue cheese

DRESSING

3 tablespoons white wine vinegar

Salt and freshly ground pepper to taste

6 tablespoons vegetable or canola oil

Cook the potatoes according to the Master Recipe (page 16) for boiling potatoes. When cool enough to handle, peel and cut into $1/2$-inch cubes. The cubes of steak and potatoes should be the same size. Place the potatoes in a large bowl and sprinkle with the vinegar while still warm.

To make the dressing, in a small bowl, whisk together the vinegar, salt, and pepper, then whisk in the oil.

Pour the dressing over the potatoes, setting the empty dressing bowl to one side. Add the onion and parsley to the potatoes and toss gently.

Put the steak cubes in the bowl in which you mixed the dressing and sprinkle the steak sauce over them. Stir to coat the cubes. Add this to the potato mixture and mix gently.

Turn the potato-steak mixture into a salad bowl and sprinkle the blue cheese over the top. Serve immediately, or cover and refrigerate the salad for up to 4 hours. Bring to room temperature before serving.

Tarragon Lamb Potato Salad

I LOVE ROAST LAMB, BUT I MUST CONFESS THAT THE LEFTOVERS PRESENT MORE OF A CHALLENGE THAN A PIECE OF ROAST BEEF DOES. A TASTY ALTERNATIVE TO SHEPHERD'S PIE, THIS SALAD IS A DELICIOUS USE OF LEFTOVER LAMB. IF THE LAMB HAS BEEN CHARCOAL GRILLED, CUT AWAY ANY BLACKENED AREAS BEFORE CUBING IT.

SERVES 6

2 pounds Red Bliss or red new potatoes

2 tablespoons tarragon vinegar

Salt to taste

About 1 cup cubed, well-trimmed roast lamb ($\frac{1}{2}$-inch cubes)

DRESSING

2 tablespoons minced shallot

1 tablespoon chopped fresh tarragon, or 1 teaspoon dried tarragon, crumbled (see note)

1 tablespoon chopped fresh flat-leaf or curly parsley

2 tablespoons tarragon vinegar

1 tablespoon Dijon mustard

Salt and freshly ground pepper to taste

6 tablespoons extra-virgin olive oil

Cook the potatoes according to the Master Recipe (page 16) for steaming potatoes. When cool enough to handle, peel if desired, then cut into $\frac{1}{2}$-inch cubes. The cubes of potato and lamb should be the same size. Place the potatoes in a large bowl. Sprinkle with the vinegar and salt while still warm. Add the lamb.

To make the dressing, in a small bowl, stir together the shallot, tarragon, parsley, vinegar, mustard, salt, and pepper. Whisk in the olive oil until an emulsion forms.

Pour the dressing over the potato-lamb mixture and mix gently but thoroughly. Serve immediately, or cover and refrigerate for up to 4 hours. Bring to room temperature before serving.

NOTE If you do not care for the slightly sharp taste of tarragon, you may substitute fresh mint for it. Do not use dried mint, however, as it has a dull flavor. If you are using fresh mint, use cider vinegar instead of the tarragon vinegar in the same amount.

Sweet Potato and Smoked Turkey Salad

I FIRST INTRODUCED MY COOKING CLASSES TO THIS UNUSUAL AND TASTY SALAD DURING THE HOLIDAY SEASON, AND IT WAS AN IMMEDIATE HIT. IT IS ADAPTED FROM A RECIPE BY THE VERY TALENTED FOOD WRITER SHARON TYLER HERBST, FROM HER INFORMATIVE BOOK *COOKING SMART*. THE SALAD CAN BE PREPARED UP TO 1 DAY IN ADVANCE, AND IT HOLDS WELL ON A BUFFET TABLE. LEFTOVER ROAST TURKEY CAN BE USED IN PLACE OF SMOKED.

SERVES 6 TO 8

1½ pounds small sweet potatoes
(6 to 8 ounces each)
2 cups cubed smoked turkey
(¼-inch cubes) (see note)
1 cup diced celery
¾ cup coarsely chopped pecans, toasted
(page 17)
¼ cup finely chopped fresh flat-leaf parsley

DRESSING

⅔ cup canola or other vegetable oil
2 tablespoons red wine vinegar
3 tablespoons fresh orange juice
3 tablespoons finely grated orange zest
2 teaspoons minced fresh ginger
½ teaspoon curry powder
½ teaspoon salt

Preheat the oven to 400°F. Scrub the sweet potatoes with a stiff brush but do not peel. Prick in several places with the tines of a fork. Bake just until tender when pierced with a fork, about 30 minutes. The timing will depend on the size of the potatoes. Alternatively, scrub and prick the potatoes and microwave on high for 6 to 8 minutes. Remove from the microwave, cover with aluminum foil, and let stand for 5 minutes. Do not overcook, or they won't cut nicely. Let cool completely, then peel and cut into ½-inch cubes. Place the cubes in a large bowl.

To make the dressing, combine all of the dressing ingredients in a blender, food processor, or jar. Process or shake for 30 seconds. You should have about 1 cup.

Add the turkey, celery, and from ¾ to 1 cup of the dressing to the cubed sweet potatoes and toss gently. Cover and refrigerate for at least 1 hour or for up to 1 day.

Just before serving, add the pecans and parsley and toss well. Serve chilled.

NOTE Smoked turkey is found in delicatessens and in the deli department of supermarkets. Ask for a single piece weighing ½ pound, or as close to that weight as possible. It will be easier to cube.

New Hampshire Mapled Ham and Potato Salad

IN NEW HAMPSHIRE, MAPLE SYRUP FINDS ITS WAY INTO MANY DISHES. THE SYRUP IS GRADED LIGHT, MEDIUM, OR DARK. LIGHT IS THE PREFERRED SYRUP OF CHOICE FOR PANCAKES AND WAFFLES, WHILE MEDIUM, BECAUSE OF ITS STRONGER FLAVOR, IS USED IN RECIPES BY MANY NEW ENGLAND COOKS. DARK IS USED COMMERCIALLY AS A FLAVORING IN OTHER PRODUCTS. THE RICH MAPLE FLAVOR OF THE SYRUP HAS A NATURAL AFFINITY WITH HAM, AS ILLUSTRATED BY THIS HEARTY FALL SALAD.

SERVES 6 TO 8

2 pounds Red Bliss or red new potatoes

2 tablespoons cider vinegar

2 to 3 scallions, including some of
the tender green tops, thinly sliced

1/2 teaspoon salt

1/4 teaspoon freshly ground pepper

1/2 pound high-quality baked ham,
in one piece, cut into 1/2-inch cubes

1/2 cup sliced radishes

DRESSING

3/4 cup mayonnaise, either homemade
(page 19) or high-quality purchased

1 tablespoon honey mustard

3 tablespoons maple syrup,
preferably Medium grade

Cook the potatoes according to the Master Recipe (page 16) for steaming potatoes. When cool enough to handle, peel if desired, then cut into 1/2-inch cubes. Place in a large bowl and sprinkle with the vinegar while still warm. Add the scallions, salt, and pepper.

To make the dressing, in a small bowl, stir together the mayonnaise, mustard, and maple syrup to taste.

Pour the dressing over potatoes. Add the ham and the radishes and toss together gently but thoroughly. Serve immediately, or cover and refrigerate for up to 1 day. Bring to room temperature before serving.

Smoked Oyster Potato Salad

YOU EITHER LOVE THE LITTLE MORSELS IN THE FLAT TINS OR YOU DON'T! THERE IS NO MIDDLE GROUND. FOR THOSE WHO FALL INTO THE FORMER CAMP, HERE IS A RECIPE THAT IS QUICK AND EASILY MANAGED WITH INGREDIENTS USUALLY ON HAND. THIS SALAD IS PARTICULARLY NICE ON A HOLIDAY BUFFET TABLE.

SERVES 6 TO 8

2 pounds Yukon Gold potatoes

2 tablespoons white wine vinegar

¼ cup chopped scallions, including tender green tops

¼ cup chopped red onion

¼ cup finely chopped fresh flat-leaf parsley

2 tablespoons chopped, roasted red bell peppers, home roasted (see note) or high-quality purchased

3 to 4 tablespoons extra-virgin olive oil

2 tins (4 ounces each) smoked oysters, drained and liquid reserved

Salt and freshly ground pepper to taste

Cook the potatoes according to the Master Recipe (page 16) for steaming potatoes. When cool enough to handle, peel and cut into pieces the same size as the oysters you are using. (This way the oysters won't get lost in the salad.) Place the potatoes in a bowl and sprinkle with the vinegar while still warm.

Add the scallions, red onion, parsley, bell peppers, and 3 tablespoons of the olive oil to the potatoes and toss gently. Add the oysters, 1½ tablespoons of the liquid drained from the oysters, the salt, and pepper.

Toss gently again, being careful not to break the oysters. If the mixture seems too dry, add the remaining 1 tablespoon olive oil.

Cover and refrigerate until serving. Bring to room temperature and stir gently before serving.

NOTE To roast the peppers, halve lengthwise and remove the stem, seeds, and ribs. Preheat a broiler. Place the pepper halves, cut-side down, on a baking sheet lined with aluminum foil. Place under the broiler, and broil until the entire surface of the pepper halves is blackened and blistered. Alternatively, if you have a gas flame, leave the pepper whole and spear it on a long fork. Char the pepper over the open flame, turning it to blacken and blister evenly. Transfer the blackened pepper to a paper or a plastic bag, close, and let stand for about 10 minutes. Remove the peppers from the bag and peel away the charred skin. Use as directed in the recipe, or wrap in plastic wrap and refrigerate for up to 2 days. Alternatively, place in a container, add olive oil to cover, and store in the refrigerator for up 1 week.

Fabulous Fourth Salmon and Potato Salad

IN NEW ENGLAND, SALMON, PEAS, AND NEW POTATOES MAKE UP THE TRADITIONAL FOURTH OF JULY MEAL. AT MY HOME, WATCH HILL, THIS VERSION OF THE TRADITIONAL FEAST COMBINES THE THREE KEY ELEMENTS IN ONE DO-AHEAD DISH, LEAVING ME FREE TO ENJOY THE FESTIVITIES WITH FAMILY AND FRIENDS. WHILE MAKING THIS DISH WITH FROZEN PEAS IS ONE OPTION, THE FLAVOR AND TEXTURE OF JUST-SHELLED FRESH PEAS CAN'T BE BEAT. YOU MAY DRESS THE POTATOES AND ADD THE SALMON SEVERAL HOURS PRIOR TO SERVING, BUT DO NOT ADD THE PEAS AND RADISHES UNTIL JUST PRIOR TO SERVING, AS THEY WILL DISCOLOR DUE TO THE ACIDITY OF THE LEMON JUICE.

SERVES 8 TO 10

2 pounds Red Bliss or red new potatoes
1 cup shelled green peas
2 pounds salmon steaks, poached and flaked (see note)
1/2 cup sliced radishes
Lettuce leaves, red-leaf or Bibb
4 hard-boiled eggs, quartered

DRESSING

1/4 cup fresh lemon juice
1/4 cup chopped fresh dill
1 shallot, thinly sliced
Salt and freshly ground pepper to taste
1/2 cup extra-virgin olive oil

Cook the potatoes according to the Master Recipe (page 16) for boiling potatoes. When cool enough to handle, peel if desired, then cut into 1/4-inch-thick slices. Place the potato slices in a large bowl and set aside.

To make the dressing, in a small bowl, whisk the lemon juice, dill, shallot, salt, and pepper. Gradually whisk in the oil until an emulsion forms. Pour the dressing over the potatoes and toss gently.

Bring a saucepan three-fourths full of water to a boil. Add the peas and boil just until tender, between 2 to 4 minutes depending on the size. Drain and immediately place under running cold water to set the color. Drain well.

Add the flaked salmon, peas, and radishes to the potatoes and toss again.

Line a large serving platter with the lettuce leaves. Spoon on the salad and garnish with the hard-boiled eggs. Serve at once.

NOTE To poach the salmon, place 1/4 teaspoon dried tarragon or 1 teaspoon fresh tarragon leaves, 1/4 teaspoon dried thyme or 1 teaspoon fresh thyme leaves, 4 or 5 sprigs of fresh flat-leaf parsley, 1 bay leaf, and 4 or 5 whole black peppercorns on a square of cheesecloth, bring the corners together, and tie securely to make a bouquet garni. In a wide stainless steel or enamel pan, combine 3/4 cup each white wine and water, 1 teaspoon salt, and the bouquet garni. Bring to a boil, reduce the heat to medium, cover partially, and simmer for 10 minutes. Add the salmon steaks and additional water if needed just to cover. Butter one side of a piece of wax paper cut to the diameter of the pan and place, buttered-side down, over the salmon. Poach at a bare simmer just until the steaks flake when tested with a fork, about 10 minutes. Remove the salmon from the liquid and let cool. Remove and discard any skin and bones, then flake with a fork.

Lobster Roll Potato Salad

WHAT CONSTITUTES A GOOD LOBSTER ROLL IN NEW ENGLAND IS AS HOTLY CONTESTED AS WHAT GOES INTO THE BEST POTATO SALAD. THE PURISTS STATE ONLY LOBSTER MEAT (AND CLAW MEAT AT THAT!) AND A MINIMUM OF MAYONNAISE SHOULD BE INCLUDED. FOR SOME, THE INCLUSION OF CELERY OR ONION IS HERESY, AND EVEN LETTUCE IS REGARDED WITH SUSPICION. REPUTATIONS HAVE RISEN OR FALLEN ON THE TREATMENT OF THE ROLL AS WELL. AGAIN, THE PURISTS HOLD STRONG VIEWS: THE ROLL SHOULD BE LIGHTLY GRILLED IN BUTTER, AND ONLY A SOFT, HOT-DOG–TYPE ROLL WILL DO. I'VE USED POTATOES INSTEAD OF A ROLL IN THIS RECIPE—A HAPPY COMPROMISE FOR ALL PARTIES.

SERVES 6 TO 8

2 pounds Red Bliss or red new potatoes
2 tablespoons white wine vinegar
¾ cup mayonnaise, homemade (page 19)
　or any high-quality purchased
½ cup diced celery
¼ cup diced red onion
1½ cups diced cooked lobster meat
Salt and freshly ground pepper to taste
Lettuce leaves
1 or 2 lobster claws, shelled (optional)

Cook the potatoes according to the Master Recipe (page 16) for boiling potatoes. When cool enough to handle, peel if desired. (If you are using small red new potatoes, it is more attractive to leave them unpeeled.) Cut into ¼-inch cubes and place in a bowl. Sprinkle the potatoes with the vinegar while still warm.

Add the mayonnaise, celery, onion, and lobster meat to the potatoes and mix gently but thoroughly. Season with salt and pepper.

Line a platter with the lettuce leaves. Arrange the salad on the leaves and garnish with the claw(s), if using. Serve immediately, or cover and refrigerate for up to 6 hours, then serve chilled.

Smoked Trout and Potato Salad

IN OUR AREA, WE HAVE A WEEKLY VISIT FROM ROBBY GRAHAM OF WARREN, MAINE, WHO BRINGS US THE FRESHEST FISH THIS SIDE OF ANYWHERE. A TRUE SON OF MAINE, HE IS SHORT ON WORDS BUT DEAD TO THE POINT. ONE OF MY FAVORITE ROBBYISMS IS, "IF THAT FISH WERE ANY FRESHER, BARBARA, IT'D NEED A SEAT BELT!" ON FRIDAYS, HIS TRUCK IS PARKED NEXT TO ROUTE 25, RAIN OR SHINE, SUMMER OR WINTER. HIS COMMENT ON BUYING FISH FROM A TRUCK: "HOW DO THOSE FOLKS THINK IT GETS TO THE SUPERMARKET, BY HELICOPTER?" IT'S BEST TO ARRIVE EARLY, AS HE SELLS OUT OF SOME OF THE FAVORITES, PARTICULARLY WHEN THE SUMMER RESIDENTS ARE AMONG US. ALONG WITH FIRST-RATE SWORD-FISH, LOBSTERS, SCALLOPS, AND SOLE, HE SELLS FANTASTIC SMOKED TROUT, BOTH PLAIN AND PEPPERED. I OFFER THE TROUT PLAIN ON CRACKERS, IN FRITTATAS, OR I MAKE LUSCIOUS SPREADS WITH CREAM CHEESE AND SOUR CREAM. I SERVE THIS ELEGANT SALAD, SUITABLE FOR ENTERTAINING, AS A FIRST COURSE OR WITH A BOWL OF ROBBY'S MUSSELS STEAMED IN WINE.

SERVES 4 TO 6

1 pound fingerling potatoes

2 tablespoons dry white wine

1/4 cup walnut oil

2 tablespoons chopped scallions, including tender green tops

1 tablespoon chopped fresh dill, or 1 teaspoon dried dill, crumbled

Salt and freshly ground pepper to taste

2 smoked trout, filleted and flesh flaked (about 1/2 pound)

Boston lettuce leaves

2 tablespoons chopped walnuts, toasted (page 17)

DRESSING

1/4 cup sour cream

1/4 cup mayonnaise, homemade (page 19) or high-quality purchased

1 to 2 teaspoons fresh lemon juice

Cook the potatoes according to the Master Recipe (page 16) for steaming potatoes. When cool enough to handle, slice the potatoes into 1/4-inch-thick slices. (I prefer not to peel the thin skin of the fingerlings, a time-consuming and unnecessary task.) Place the potatoes in a large bowl and sprinkle with the white wine and walnut oil while still warm. Toss gently. Add the scallions and dill, and toss gently again. Season with the salt and pepper. (If you are using the peppered trout, omit the pepper.)

To make the dressing, in a small bowl, whisk together the sour cream, mayonnaise, and lemon juice.

Add the smoked trout and the dressing to the potatoes. Toss gently, being careful not to break up the potatoes. Line a platter with the lettuce leaves. Arrange the salad on the greens and sprinkle with the walnuts.

Serve at once, or cover and refrigerate for up to 6 hours, then serve chilled.

Crabmeat and Potato Salad

THIS RECIPE CAME ABOUT ONE DAY WHEN I MENTIONED TO ROBBY GRAHAM, MY FISH PURVEYOR, THAT THE COOKBOOK ON POTATO SALADS WAS COMING ALONG, AND I WAS WORKING ON THE SEAFOOD SALAD SECTION. "GOT ONE FOR CRAB?" ROBBY ASKED. I TOLD HIM I DIDN'T. "WELL, OUR FRESH MAINE CRAB CAN'T BE BEAT," HE SAID, AS HE TUCKED A CONTAINER IN WITH MY WEEKLY PURCHASE. IF YOU CANNOT FIND FRESH CRABMEAT, YOU MAY SUBSTITUTE CANNED OF GOOD QUALITY. AND IF YOU'RE EVER IN NEW ENGLAND, TRY THE MAINE CRAB ALONG WITH THE LOBSTERS.

SERVES 4 TO 6

1 pound Yukon Gold potatoes

3 1/2 tablespoons fresh lemon juice

1 cup well-drained, chopped canned or cooked frozen artichoke hearts

1/2 pound fresh-cooked crabmeat or 2 cans (6 ounces each) canned crabmeat, drained, picked over for cartilage and shell fragments, and flaked

DRESSING

1 cup mayonnaise, homemade (page 19) or high-quality purchased

2 tablespoons capers, rinsed

1 tablespoon chopped fresh flat-leaf or curly parsley

2 scallions, including some of the tender green tops, chopped

1 clove garlic, minced

1 tablespoon minced fresh tarragon, or 1 teaspoon dried tarragon, crumbled

1/2 teaspoon dry mustard

1/4 to 1/2 teaspoon Tabasco or other hot-pepper sauce

Dash of salt

1/4 teaspoon paprika

Cook the potatoes according to the Master Recipe (page 16) for boiling potatoes. When cool enough to handle, peel and cut into 1/4-inch cubes. Place in a large bowl and sprinkle with 2 tablespoons of the lemon juice while still warm. Cover and refrigerate while making the dressing.

To make the dressing, in a bowl, combine the mayonnaise, capers, parsley, scallions, garlic, tarragon, dry mustard, hot-pepper sauce, salt, and paprika. Stir to mix thoroughly.

Toss the artichoke hearts with the remaining 1 1/2 tablespoons of lemon juice and add to the dressing. Add the crabmeat and toss gently.

Remove the potatoes from the refrigerator (they should be cool to the touch) and add the crabmeat-artichoke mixture. Toss gently but thoroughly. Serve immediately, or cover and refrigerate for up to 6 hours, then serve chilled.

NOTE This salad is attractive packed into 6 custard cups that have been lightly sprayed with vegetable oil spray, tamped down, and refrigerated. Cover the cups with plastic wrap. When ready to serve, place a lettuce leaf on each individual plate and top with a large, perfect tomato slice. Unmold the cups onto the tomato slices. Garnish each salad with a tarragon sprig and a few capers.

Sunday Morning Smoked Salmon Potato Salad | ONE OF LIFE'S GREAT

PLEASURES IS A SUMMER SUNDAY MORNING ON MY FRONT PORCH OVERLOOKING LAKE WINNIPESAUKEE. FIRST, I MAKE A SHORT TRIP TO WINNIPESAUKEE BAY GULLS, THE LOCAL BAGEL SHOP. THEN I LAY THE TABLE WITH FRAGRANT TOASTED BAGELS, CREAM CHEESE, SOME SLICED RED ONION, A SMALL POT OF CAPERS, AND A GENEROUS AMOUNT OF FRESHLY SMOKED SALMON FROM ROBBY GRAHAM'S GEORGE'S RIVER SEAFOOD. STRONG FRESH COFFEE, THE *BOSTON GLOBE*, AND THE *NEW YORK TIMES* COMPLETE THE SCENE. IF THERE'S SALMON LEFT, THIS SALAD WILL BE SERVED FOR SUNDAY LUNCH.

SERVES 6 TO 8

2 pounds Red Bliss or red new potatoes

2 tablespoons champagne vinegar or
 white wine vinegar

¼ cup finely chopped red onion

1 tablespoon capers, rinsed

1 tablespoon finely chopped fresh tarragon,
 or 1 teaspoon dried tarragon, crumbled

8 to 12 ounces smoked salmon or lox,
 cut into ¼-inch-wide julienne strips

DRESSING

⅓ cup mayonnaise, homemade (page 19)
 or high-quality purchased

⅓ cup sour cream, full fat or low fat

1 tablespoon champagne vinegar or
 white wine vinegar

Salt and freshly ground pepper to taste

Cook the potatoes according to the Master Recipe (page 16) for steaming potatoes. When cool enough to handle, peel and cut into ¼-inch cubes. Place in a large bowl and sprinkle with the vinegar while still warm. Let cool to room temperature. Add the onion, capers, tarragon, and smoked salmon to the cooled potatoes and toss very gently but thoroughly.

To make the dressing, in a small bowl, stir together the mayonnaise, sour cream, vinegar, salt, and pepper. Pour the dressing over the potato mixture and toss gently but thoroughly. Serve immediately, or cover and refrigerate for up to 4 hours, then serve chilled.

Potato Salad Molly Malone

IF YOU'VE EVER BEEN TO THE "FAIR CITY" OF DUBLIN AND WALKED THE "STREETS BROAD AND NARROW," I'M SURE YOU'VE HUMMED THE TUNE ABOUT MOLLY MALONE AND HER WHEELBARROW ALIVE WITH COCKLES AND MUSSELS. WELL, THE COCKLES MAY BE HARD TO COME BY, BUT MUSSELS ARE BECOMING INCREASING POPULAR IN THIS COUNTRY. INEXPENSIVE, NUTRITIOUS, AND LOW IN CALORIES, THESE TASTY MOLLUSKS COME TOGETHER WITH ANOTHER IRISH FAVORITE, POTATOES, TO MAKE A SALAD FOR WHICH EVEN SWEET MOLLY WOULD CROSS THE RIVER LIFFEY.

SERVES 6 TO 8

2 pounds mussels
1/2 cup water
1/2 cup dry white wine
1 clove garlic, smashed but not peeled
2 pounds Red Bliss or red new potatoes
1/3 cup diced red onion
1/2 cup diced fennel (see note)
1/4 cup chopped fresh flat-leaf or
    curly parsley

DRESSING

2 teaspoons Dijon mustard, preferably
    whole grain
2 tablespoons white wine vinegar
1 teaspoon salt
1/4 teaspoon freshly ground pepper
1/4 cup extra-virgin olive oil

To prepare the mussels, scrub them with a stiff brush to remove any sand or grit. Remove any protruding beards (the dark fibrous matter, resembling Spanish moss, that protrudes from the seam where the shells meet). Discard any mussels that do not close to the touch or are cracked.

Place the water, wine, and garlic clove in the bottom of a pot, preferably one with a removable steamer basket. Place the mussels in the basket, if using, or directly in the bottom of the pot. Cover, bring to a boil, and cook until the mussels open, about 5 minutes. Lift the mussels from the pot, discarding any that have failed to open. Remove the meats from the shells and place them in a bowl. Sprinkle them with a few tablespoons of the mussel cooking liquid, making sure not to scoop up any sand that may have settled to the bottom of the pan. Set aside.

Cook the potatoes according to the Master Recipe (page 16) for steaming potatoes. When cool enough to handle, peel them if desired, then cut into 1/2-inch-thick slices. Place the potato slices in a large bowl.

Add the mussels, red onion, fennel, and parsley to the potatoes while still warm. Toss gently but thoroughly.

To make the dressing, in a small bowl, whisk together the mustard, vinegar, salt, and pepper. Slowly whisk in the olive oil until an emulsion forms.

Pour the dressing over the potato-mussel mixture and toss gently but thoroughly. Serve immediately, or cover and refrigerate for up to 1 day. Bring to room temperature before serving.

NOTE Fennel, sometimes called finocchio or Florence fennel, has a pale green to white bulbous end, long stems, and dark green feathery leaves. Cut off the long stems and fronds. Cut the bulb in half lengthwise. Cut a V in the root end of each half to remove the core. Chop what you need for the salad and refrigerate the rest. Fennel is delicious on a crudités platter or as a crunchy addition to other salads. The feathery tops make an attractive garnish.

Jo's Asian Potato Salad

MY SISTER, JO, HAS BEEN PART OF A BOOK CLUB THAT HAS BEEN MEETING FOR YEARS. SUPPER IS ALWAYS A HIGHLIGHT OF THESE LITERARY GATHERINGS. WORD OF MOUTH AND PASSED-ON RECIPES ARE SOMETIMES THE BEST. JO VOLUNTEERED THIS LONGTIME FAVORITE AS ONE THAT EVEN *THE KITCHEN GOD'S WIFE* WOULD SURELY ENJOY!

SERVES 6

12 whole scallions, plus 5 tablespoons minced scallion, white part only

1/2 cup canola oil

1/4 cup Asian sesame oil

2 pounds new potatoes

5 tablespoons minced prosciutto (see note)

3 tablespoons rice vinegar

3/4 teaspoon freshly ground pepper

1/2 teaspoon salt

1/3 cup chopped cashews, toasted (page 17)

Trim off the roots and the tough green tops of the whole scallions. Using a Chinese cleaver or a large, wide-bladed knife, flatten 12 scallions on a work surface.

Combine the canola and sesame oils in a skillet over high heat. Cover and cook the oils just until they begin to smoke, 2 to 4 minutes. Remove the skillet from the heat. Add the flattened scallions to the hot oils, cover, and let stand for 30 minutes.

Meanwhile, cook the potatoes according to the Master Recipe (page 16) for steaming potatoes. When cool enough to handle, peel, cut into 1/2-inch-thick slices, and place in a large bowl.

Pour the contents of the skillet into a sieve set over a bowl, and press on the scallions with the back of a spoon to extract as much oil as possible. Add the prosciutto, 3 tablespoons of the minced scallion, the vinegar, pepper, and salt to the oil and stir just to combine.

Pour the oil mixture over the potatoes, toss gently, cover, and let stand at room temperature for 3 hours before serving. (The salad can also be prepared up to 1 day in advance, covered, and refrigerated.)

Just before serving, sprinkle the cashews over the salad and toss gently. Sprinkle the remaining 2 tablespoons scallions over the salad. Serve chilled or at room temperature.

NOTE Prosciutto may not seem like a very Asian ingredient, but the authentic Yunnan and Jinhua hams are not sold in this country. Smithfield ham may also be used, but prosciutto is more readily available.

Alpine Potato and Cheese Salad

WHEN MY FAMILY LIVED IN EUROPE, WE SPENT MOST OF OUR VACATIONS SKIING IN THE SWISS OR AUSTRIAN ALPS. ONE DAY, AFTER A PARTICULARLY HORRENDOUS RUN, I TOOK OFF MY SKIS, PLUNGED THEM IN A SNOW BANK, AND SAID, "THAT'S IT! NEVER AGAIN. LIFE IS TOO SHORT TO BE COLD AND TERRIFIED ON VACATION!" THEREAFTER, MY MISSION WAS TO FIND THE EVENING'S RESTAURANT. I WOULD PERUSE MENUS, AND IF I THOUGHT THE PLACE WOULD APPEAL TO THE REST OF THE FAMILY, I WOULD MAKE THE RESERVATION. THESE EXPLORATIONS LED TO THE DISCOVERY OF THE BAKERIES, *KONDITOREI*, AND WURST AND CHEESE SHOPS IN THE VILLAGES. OF COURSE, SOME TASTING WAS INVOLVED. HERE IS ONE OF MY FAVORITE SWISS SALADS.

SERVES 6

2 pounds red or brown all-purpose potatoes

2 tablespoons white wine vinegar

Salt and freshly ground pepper to taste

2 cups cubed Emmenthaler, Gruyère, or other good-quality Swiss cheese (¼-inch cubes)

2 cups diced celery

Green-leaf lettuce leaves

½ cup coarsely chopped walnuts, toasted (page 17)

DRESSING

1 cup mayonnaise, homemade (page 19) or high-quality purchased

1 tablespoon Dijon mustard, preferably whole grain

1 tablespoon Worcestershire sauce

Cook the potatoes according to the Master Recipe (page 16) for boiling potatoes. When cool enough to handle, peel, cut into ¼-inch cubes, and place in a large bowl. Sprinkle with the vinegar, salt, and pepper while still warm and let cool to room temperature. Add the cheese and celery to the cooled potatoes. Toss gently but thoroughly.

To make the dressing, in a small bowl, stir together the mayonnaise, mustard, and Worcestershire sauce. Add the dressing to the potato mixture and stir gently but thoroughly.

Salad may be covered and refrigerated for up to 2 days. When ready to serve, line a bowl with the lettuce leaves. Pile the potato mixture on the greens and sprinkle with the walnuts. Serve chilled.

An Irish Potato Salad

IN SOUTHIE, AS BOSTON'S HISTORICALLY IRISH NEIGHBORHOOD HAS LONG BEEN KNOWN, THE ANNUAL ST. PATRICK'S DAY PARADE IS A MUCH-ANTICIPATED EVENT. THE DATE IS ALSO KNOWN AS EVACUATION DAY, IN COMMEMORATION OF THE DAY THE BRITISH LEFT THE TOWN, AND IT IS A FULL-BLOWN HOLIDAY. CORNED BEEF AND CABBAGE IS THE TYPICAL FARE SERVED ON THAT DAY. IN THIS CELEBRATORY SALAD, DENNY'S BOILED DRESSING BINDS THE TRADITIONAL CORNED BEEF TOGETHER WITH OTHER INGREDIENTS. THE DRESSING IS NAMED FOR DENNY STRINGFELLOW, WHOSE GRANDMOTHER CREATED THE RECIPE AND WHOSE GREAT-GRANDMOTHER WAS FROM IRELAND. DENNY IS A STUDENT IN MY NEW HAMPSHIRE COOKING CLASSES, AN EXPERT QUILTER, AND A GOOD FRIEND. ☉ YOU WILL END UP WITH MORE DRESSING THAN YOU NEED TO DRESS THIS SALAD. STORE THE REMAINDER IN THE REFRIGERATOR FOR UP TO 3 DAYS AND USE TO MAKE COLESLAW OR A MIXED VEGETABLE SALAD, OR POUR IT OVER SLICED TOMATOES AND CUCUMBERS.

SERVES 6 TO 8

DENNY'S BOILED DRESSING

1 large egg, lightly beaten
1/2 cup sugar
1 tablespoon flour
1/2 cup cider vinegar
1/2 teaspoon salt
1/4 teaspoon freshly ground pepper
2 tablespoons butter
2 cups mayonnaise, homemade (page 19) or high-quality purchased.

2 1/2 pounds Red Bliss potatoes
2 tablespoons white wine vinegar
1/4 cup chopped pickled sweet onions
1 tablespoon celery seed
1/2 cup chopped scallions, including tender green tops
1 cup chopped celery
1 1/2 cups diced cooked corned beef
Salt and freshly ground pepper to taste

To make the dressing, in a small saucepan, stir the egg and sugar to combine. Stir in the flour until well blended, then add the cider vinegar. Add the salt, pepper, and butter and place over medium heat.

Bring to a boil, stirring occasionally. Adjust the heat to maintain a gentle boil and cook, stirring gently, until thickened, 10 to 12 minutes. Remove from the heat, transfer to a bowl, and let cool completely. Add the mayonnaise and stir to combine. You should have about 3 cups of dressing.

Cook the potatoes according to the Master Recipe (see page 16) for boiling potatoes. When cool enough to handle,

peel if desired, then cut into 1/2-inch cubes. Place in a large bowl and add the wine vinegar, pickled onions, and celery seed. Toss gently to blend.

Add the scallions, chopped celery, and corned beef and season with salt and pepper. (Be careful how much salt you add, as corned beef can be quite salty.) Add 3/4 cup of the dressing and mix gently. Add more dressing as needed to bind the salad ingredients. Cover the salad and refrigerate for up to 2 days. Serve chilled.

Greek Potato Salad

THE GREEKS LOVE THEIR POTATOES. HERE IS MY VERSION OF A GREEK SUMMER POTATO SALAD, SERVED WARM, WITH A FRAGRANT HERB DRESSING. IF YOU ARE MAKING THIS SALAD AHEAD AND REFRIGERATING IT, BRING IT TO ROOM TEMPERATURE BEFORE SERVING.

SERVES 6

2 pounds Red Bliss potatoes

1 bunch scallions, including tender green tops, finely chopped

2/3 cup Kalamata olives, pitted and roughly chopped

2/3 cup crumbled feta cheese

2/3 cup peeled, seeded, and diced cucumber

1 tomato, seeded and diced

Chopped fresh flat-leaf or curly parsley for garnish

DRESSING

3 tablespoons white wine vinegar or fresh lemon juice

1 teaspoon dried oregano, crumbled

Salt and freshly ground pepper to taste

6 tablespoons extra-virgin olive oil

Cook the potatoes according to the Master Recipe (page 16) for steaming potatoes. When cool enough to handle, peel and slice immediately into 1/4-inch-thick slices. Place in a bowl and add the scallions, olives, feta cheese, cucumber, and tomato while still warm. Mix gently.

To make the dressing, in a small bowl, whisk together the vinegar or lemon juice, oregano, salt, and pepper. Gradually whisk in the olive oil until an emulsion forms.

Pour the dressing over the potato mixture and toss gently but thoroughly.

Garnish the salad with the parsley. Serve at once while still warm. Or, cover and refrigerate for up to 6 hours, then bring to room temperature before serving.

THE INTERNATIONALS

Pesto Potato Salad

WHILE THERE ARE ACCEPTABLE PESTOS IN JARS, TUBES, AND EVEN "FRESH" AT THE DELI COUNTER IN SUPERMARKETS, THEY CANNOT MATCH HOMEMADE. PESTO IS TRADITIONALLY MADE WITH A MORTAR AND PESTLE, BUT THE ADVENT OF THE FOOD PROCESSOR HAS SIMPLIFIED THE TASK. WHEN THE FRAGRANT SAUCE IS COMBINED WITH POTATOES, PASTA, AND GREEN BEANS, A WONDERFUL DISH IS CREATED. IN GENOA, WHERE PESTO ORIGINATED, THE SAUCE IS USED TO DRESS A HOMEMADE CURLY-EDGED PASTA CALLED TRENETTE THAT IS SIMILAR TO FETTUCCINE. FOR THIS SALAD I HAVE CHOSEN FUSILLI, A CORKSCREW-SHAPED PASTA THAT TRAPS THE BITS OF THE SAUCE IN ITS RIDGES.

SERVES 6 TO 8

PESTO

2 cups loosely packed fresh basil leaves, thoroughly dried

$\frac{1}{2}$ cup extra-virgin olive oil, or as needed

3 cloves garlic

$\frac{1}{2}$ cup pine nuts or walnuts

$\frac{1}{2}$ cup freshly grated Parmesan cheese

Salt to taste

2 pounds Yukon Gold potatoes

2 tablespoons white wine vinegar

$\frac{1}{4}$ cup chicken stock

1 cup cooled cooked fusilli pasta

1 cup cut-up green beans ($\frac{1}{2}$-inch lengths), boiled until tender, drained, and cooled

To make the pesto, place the basil leaves in a food processor. With the motor running, slowly add the olive oil through the feed tube and then add the garlic cloves. Stop the motor, remove the lid, add the nuts, replace the lid, and pulse the machine until the nuts are chopped and the pesto is creamy. If it is too thick, whirl in more oil. Transfer the pesto to a bowl and stir in the grated cheese. Season with salt. (Be careful, Parmesan can be very salty.) You should have about 1 cup. Measure out $\frac{1}{4}$ cup for the salad. Store the remaining pesto in a jar, topping it with a thin film of olive oil before capping. It will keep for up to 1 month in the refrigerator.

Cook the potatoes according to the Master Recipe (page 16) for boiling potatoes. When cool enough to handle, cut into $\frac{1}{4}$-inch cubes. Place in a large bowl and sprinkle with the vinegar and chicken stock while still warm. Toss gently.

Add the pasta and green beans and toss to mix. Add the $\frac{1}{4}$ cup pesto and toss gently but thoroughly. Taste and add more pesto if desired.

Serve immediately, or cover and refrigerate for up to 1 hour. Bring to room temperature before serving.

"Stop and Go" Italian Potato Salad

I CAN NEVER RESIST STOPPING AT A FARMER'S PRODUCE STAND AND FEASTING MY EYES ON THE BRILLIANT ARRAY OF COLORS ON SHOW, ESPECIALLY WHEN THE SEASON REACHES ITS PEAK IN AUGUST. ONE DAY, A GLORIOUS DISPLAY OF HUGE RED, YELLOW, AND GREEN PEPPERS, WITH THE SIGN "STOP AND GO TRAFFIC-STOPPING PEPPERS", CAUGHT MY EYE. IT WAS THE INSPIRATION FOR THIS SUMMERTIME ITALIAN ANTIPASTO-TYPE POTATO SALAD.

SERVES 6

1½ pounds red or brown
   all-purpose potatoes
2 large red bell peppers
2 large yellow bell peppers
2 large green bell peppers
Salt and freshly ground pepper to taste
4 scallions, including tender green tops,
   chopped
½ cup cubed provolone cheese
   (¼-inch cubes)
½ cup cubed salami (¼-inch cubes)
6 Italian-style black olives, pitted
6 fresh flat-leaf parsley or basil sprigs
6 red-leaf or Boston lettuce leaves

DRESSING

3 tablespoons red wine vinegar
½ teaspoon dried oregano, crumbled
Salt and freshly ground pepper to taste
6 tablespoons extra-virgin olive oil

Cook the potatoes according to the Master Recipe (page 16) for boiling potatoes. While the potatoes are cooking, cut a thin slice from the base of each bell pepper so that the pepper will stand upright. Then cut a slice off the stem end, to leave an opening large enough to permit stuffing with the potato salad later. For added color, dice the flesh from these slices, and add them to the salad when you toss it. With your fingers, remove the seeds and ribs from inside of the peppers. Sprinkle the insides with salt and pepper and turn the peppers upside down on paper towels. Let stand until you finish preparing the potato salad.

When the potatoes are cooked and cool enough to handle, peel and cut into ¼-inch cubes. Place the potato cubes in a bowl and let cool to room temperature.

To make the dressing, in a small bowl, whisk together the vinegar, oregano, salt, and pepper. Gradually whisk in the olive oil until an emulsion forms.

Add the scallions, provolone, and salami to the cooled potatoes and mix gently. Pour the dressing over all and toss gently but thoroughly. Taste and adjust the seasoning.

Turn the peppers right-side up and fill with the potato mixture. Top each filled pepper with an olive and a sprig of parsley or basil. Place a lettuce leaf on each individual plate and top with a pepper.

Serve immediately, or cover and refrigerate for up to 2 hours, then serve chilled.

Marie's French Potato Salad

I SPENT MY JUNIOR YEAR OF COLLEGE STUDYING IN PARIS, AND I LIVED WITH A DELIGHTFUL COUPLE, MONSIEUR AND MADAME JEAN LEBIDOIS, IN THEIR APARTMENT ON THE RUE DE ROME. THEY EMPLOYED MARIE, AN APPLE-CHEEKED BRETON HOUSEKEEPER, WHO WOULD ROLL THE BREAKFAST CART, LADEN WITH CAFÉ AU LAIT AND FRESH BREAD, DOWN THE LONG HALL WITH ALL THE SOLEMNITY OF A SOLDIER DRIVING A TUMBREL TO THE GUILLOTINE. IN A SONOROUS VOICE SHE WOULD ANNOUNCE, "C'EST SERVIE, MADEMOISELLE." SHE ALSO PREPARED THE NOON MEAL, AND HER POTATO SALAD WAS ONE OF MY FAVORITES. MARIE IS LONG DEPARTED, BUT THE MEMORY OF HER SIMPLE, BUT DELICIOUS, SALAD IS NOT. IT WAS MY INTRODUCTION TO POTATO SALAD WITHOUT MAYONNAISE, AND THE BEGINNING OF A LIFE-LONG LOVE AFFAIR WITH GOOD FOOD.

SERVES 6 TO 8

2 pounds red potatoes
1 small yellow onion, minced
1/4 cup chopped fresh curly parsley
2 hard-boiled eggs, quartered (optional)

VINAIGRETTE
1/4 cup white wine vinegar or cider vinegar
1 teaspoon salt
3/4 cup extra-virgin olive oil
1 tablespoon minced fresh curly parsley
1/4 teaspoon freshly ground pepper

Cook the potatoes according to the Master Recipe (page 16) for boiling potatoes. When cool enough to handle, peel and cut into 1/4-inch-thick slices. Place in a salad bowl and add the minced onion while still warm.

To make the vinaigrette, in a small bowl, whisk together the vinegar and salt to "melt" the salt. Gradually whisk in the olive oil until an emulsion forms. Whisk in the parsley and pepper.

Pour about 1/2 cup of the vinaigrette over the potatoes and toss gently but thoroughly. Add more dressing if the mixture is too dry.

If serving immediately, garnish the salad with chopped parsley, and, if you wish, with the hard-boiled eggs. Or, cover and refrigerate for up to 6 hours. Bring to room temperature and garnish before serving.

Niçoise Potato Salad

SINCE A NIÇOISE SALAD IS ONE OF MY FAVORITE SUMMER SALADS, AND POTATOES ARE ONE OF MY FAVORITE THINGS, I DECIDED TO CREATE A POTATO SALAD WITH THE FLAVORINGS OF A CLASSIC NIÇOISE. THE CHOICE OF TUNA AND OLIVES IS IMPORTANT HERE. FOR THE MOST AUTHENTIC TASTE, USE ONLY SOLID WHITE-MEAT TUNA PACKED IN OLIVE OIL AND GOOD NIÇOISE OLIVES. THE OLIVES MAY BE FOUND IN YOUR SUPERMARKET DELI OR SPECIALTY-FOOD SHOPS. IF YOU HAVE ANCHOVY DISSENTERS, LEAVE OUT THE WHOLE ANCHOVIES IN THE GARNISH, BUT DON'T OMIT THE PASTE IN THE DRESSING. IT LENDS A WONDERFULLY MYSTERIOUS FLAVOR.

SERVES 6 TO 8

2 pounds Red Bliss potatoes
½ cup cut-up young green beans
   (1-inch lengths)
2 tablespoons white wine vinegar
Salt and freshly ground pepper to taste
1 can (6 ounces) solid white-meat tuna in
   olive oil, drained and flaked

DRESSING

2 tablespoons tarragon vinegar
2 teaspoons anchovy paste
1 clove garlic, minced
⅓ cup extra-virgin olive oil

OPTIONAL GARNISHES

3 or 4 perfect fresh basil leaves
1 tomato, cut into eighths
2 hard-boiled eggs, quartered lengthwise
3 or 4 anchovy fillets in olive oil,
   drained on paper towels
1 tablespoon capers, rinsed and patted dry
½ cup black olives, preferably Niçoise, pitted

Cook the potatoes according to the Master Recipe (page 16) for steaming potatoes. Add the green beans to the steamer basket about 5 minutes before the potatoes are done. Remove the beans and potatoes and set the beans aside. When the potatoes are cool enough to handle, cut into ¼-inch-thick slices. Place in a large bowl and sprinkle with the white wine vinegar, salt, and pepper while still warm. Anchovy fillets are salty, as is the paste. Bear this in mind when adding the salt. Let the potatoes cool to room temperature.

To make the dressing, in a small bowl, whisk together the tarragon vinegar, anchovy paste, and garlic. Whisk in the olive oil until an emulsion forms.

Add the tuna and the beans to the potatoes. Pour the dressing over the potato mixture and toss gently but thoroughly.

The salad may be covered and refrigerated for a short time. (If you want to make the salad more than 30 minutes in advance, add the beans just before serving, as the acidity of the vinegar will turn the beans a dull color.) Just before serving, garnish the salad, if desired, with the basil leaves, and arrange the tomato and egg pieces and the anchovy fillets in a spoke pattern on top. Sprinkle the capers and olives over all.

Portuguese Potato Salad

THERE IS A LARGE PORTUGUESE POPULATION IN SOUTHERN NEW ENGLAND, AND THEY HAVE CONTRIBUTED RICHLY TO THE CULINARY SCENE. IN MY OPINION, SAUSAGES ARE AMONG THEIR GREATEST CONTRIBUTIONS, WITH *LINGUIÇA* THE BEST KNOWN. IN TRYING TO DETERMINE WHICH SAUSAGE TO USE FOR THIS POTATO SALAD, I CONTACTED SEVERAL SAUSAGE MAKERS IN THE AREA AND FOUND THAT *LINGUIÇA* AND *CHOURIÇO* SAUSAGES RELY ON BASICALLY THE SAME INGREDIENTS—PORK, GARLIC, PAPRIKA—BUT VARY IN TASTE BECAUSE OF FORMULAS USED BY SAUSAGE MAKERS. *LINGUIÇA* GENERALLY HAS A MILD FLAVOR, WHILE *CHOURIÇO* IS USUALLY HOTTER. WHEN IN DOUBT, TRY A SPICY ANDOUILLE SAUSAGE OR CHOOSE WHAT YOU LIKE, DEPENDING ON YOUR HEAT TOLERANCE.

SERVES 6 TO 8

2 pounds Yukon Gold potatoes

2 tablespoons white wine vinegar

1 ½ tablespoons extra-virgin olive oil

¾ pound linguiça or chouriço *sausage, cut into ¼-inch-thick slices and slices halved*

1 cup canned garbanzo beans, rinsed and well drained

⅓ cup chopped red bell pepper

¼ cup chopped red onion

¼ cup chopped celery

2 tablespoons chopped fresh flat-leaf parsley

DRESSING

2 tablespoons white wine vinegar

Dash of salt

Freshly ground pepper to taste

1 teaspoon Dijon mustard

1 teaspoon anchovy paste

4 to 5 tablespoons extra-virgin olive oil

Cook the potatoes according to the Master Recipe (page 16) for boiling potatoes. When cool enough to handle, peel and cut into ½-inch cubes. Place in a bowl and sprinkle with the vinegar while still warm.

In a skillet over medium heat, warm the olive oil. Add the sausages and sauté until lightly browned, about 4 minutes. Using a slotted spoon, transfer to paper towels to drain.

To make the dressing, in a small bowl, whisk together the vinegar, salt, and pepper until the salt dissolves. Whisk in the mustard and anchovy paste until blended. Gradually whisk in 4 tablespoons of the

olive oil until an emulsion forms. If the dressing is too thick, whisk in the remaining 1 tablespoon olive oil. Set aside.

Add the sausages, garbanzo beans, bell pepper, onion, celery, and parsley to the potatoes. Pour the dressing over all and toss gently but thoroughly.

Serve immediately, or cover and refrigerate for up to 1 day. Bring to room temperature before serving.

Curried Potato Salad

I HAVE ALWAYS ENJOYED THE FLAVOR IMPARTED BY CURRY POWDER, AND HAVE EVEN MADE MY OWN UPON OCCASION. CURRY IS A GENERIC TERM FOR A BLEND OF GROUND DRIED SPICES USED TO SEASON A WIDE RANGE OF DISHES. SUPERMARKET BRANDS GENERALLY CONTAIN A COMBINATION OF TEN TO FIFTEEN SPICES, BUT CURRY AFICIONADOS MAY INCLUDE MANY MORE IN THEIR CUSTOM BLENDS. SOME CURRIES ARE MILD, OTHERS FIERY. THE AMOUNT OF CHILE PEPPER USED DETERMINES THE HEAT. IF YOU'VE HAD YOUR CURRY POWDER FOR A WHILE (OVER A YEAR), CONSIDER BUYING A FRESH SUPPLY FOR THIS RECIPE, AS THE FLAVOR DIMINISHES OVER TIME. JUST WAVE THE JAR UNDER YOUR NOSE: NO AROMA, NO TASTE.

SERVES 6 TO 8

2 pounds Yukon Gold potatoes

2 tablespoons rice vinegar

Salt and freshly ground pepper to taste

1/2 cup scallions, including tender green tops

1/3 cup raisins

1/4 cup chopped cashews, toasted (page 17)

DRESSING

1/2 cup mayonnaise (page 19), homemade or high-quality purchased

1/2 cup plain yogurt

2 to 3 teaspoons curry powder

2 tablespoons Major Grey chutney, chopped

Cook the potatoes according to the Master Recipe (page 16) for steaming potatoes. When cool enough to handle, peel and cut into 1/4-inch-thick slices. Place in a large bowl and sprinkle with the vinegar, salt, and pepper while still warm. Add the scallions and the raisins and toss gently.

To make the dressing, in a small bowl, combine the mayonnaise, yogurt, curry powder, and chutney. Whisk gently to blend. Pour the dressing over the potatoes and toss gently but thoroughly.

Turn into a serving bowl, cover, and refrigerate for 2 to 3 hours to blend the flavors. Just before serving, add the cashews and toss to distribute evenly. Serve chilled.

Russian Potato Salad

DID THE FRENCH AMBASSADOR HAVE THIS DISH AT THE COURT OF CATHERINE THE GREAT AND SPIRIT IT HOME INTO THE WAITING PANTRY OF FRENCH CUISINE? THE PRESENCE OF BEETS POINTS TO ITS RUSSIAN ORIGINS, AND I FIRST ENCOUNTERED THE SALAD IN FRANCE, WHERE IT GARNISHED A COLD MEAT PLATTER ON A BUFFET. I HAVE SINCE FOUND IT THROUGHOUT EUROPE, MOSTLY AVAILABLE FOR TAKEOUT IN DELICATESSENS, ALTHOUGH I HAVE SELDOM SEEN IT IN THE UNITED STATES. TRADITIONALLY MOLDED IN A DOME SHAPE, IT CAN ALSO BE SERVED ATTRACTIVELY ON A LONG LETTUCE-LINED PLATTER. YOU MAY VARY THE VEGETABLES, BUT THEY ALL SHOULD BE CUT INTO THE SAME-SIZED DICE. I HAVE GIVEN INSTRUCTIONS FOR THE CLASSIC GARNISH, BUT THE FUN PART IS DESIGNING YOUR OWN.

SERVES 6 TO 8

1 pound Red Bliss potatoes
1 cup diced cooked carrots ($\frac{1}{4}$-inch dice)
1 cup cooked peas
1 cup diced cooked red beets
($\frac{1}{4}$-inch dice; see note)
$\frac{1}{2}$ cup diced sweet onion such as Vidalia or Maui ($\frac{1}{4}$-inch dice)
$\frac{1}{2}$ cup diced celery ($\frac{1}{4}$-inch dice)
1 cup mayonnaise, homemade (page 19) or high-quality purchased
Salt and freshly ground white pepper to taste
6 to 8 leaves red leaf or Boston lettuce

GARNISH

2 hard-boiled eggs, sliced
Chopped fresh curly parsley
Anchovy fillets in olive oil, rinsed and drained on paper towels (optional)
Tongue, ham, or smoked salmon strips (optional)
Capers, rinsed (optional)
Gherkins, sliced (optional)

Cook the potatoes according to the Master Recipe (page 16) for boiling potatoes. When cool enough to handle, peel and cut into $\frac{1}{4}$-inch cubes. Place in a large bowl and let cool to room temperature.

Add the carrots, peas, beets, onion, and celery to the cooled potatoes. Add the mayonnaise, season with salt and pepper, and toss gently but thoroughly. Cover and refrigerate until serving time.

Cover a platter with the lettuce leaves and spoon the salad atop the greens. Arrange the hard-boiled eggs on the top of the salad and sprinkle the parsley between the slices. If you wish, add the anchovy fillets or the strips of tongue, ham, or smoked salmon in an attractive pattern. Top with the capers and/or gherkins, if desired. Serve immediately.

NOTE The addition of beets turns the salad a rosy pink. If you prefer to omit the beets, you may substitute a like quantity of green beans, cut into $\frac{1}{4}$-inch pieces and cooked. I find this method of cooking beets gives the sweetest results.

Preheat the oven to 400°F. Rinse as many beets as you like, but leave the skins on. Place the beets on a piece of aluminum foil, bring the edges together, and seal tightly to prevent the juice from escaping. Bake for 30 to 60 minutes, depending on the size of the beets. They are done when a knife tip pierces them easily. Open the packet carefully, as the hot steam and juice will escape, and remove the beets. Run the beets under cold water and slip off the skins. Use immediately, or store in the refrigerator for up to 2 days. You can reheat the cooked beets by wrapping them in foil and placing in a preheated 350°F oven for 15 minutes.

SOME LIKE IT HOT: PO

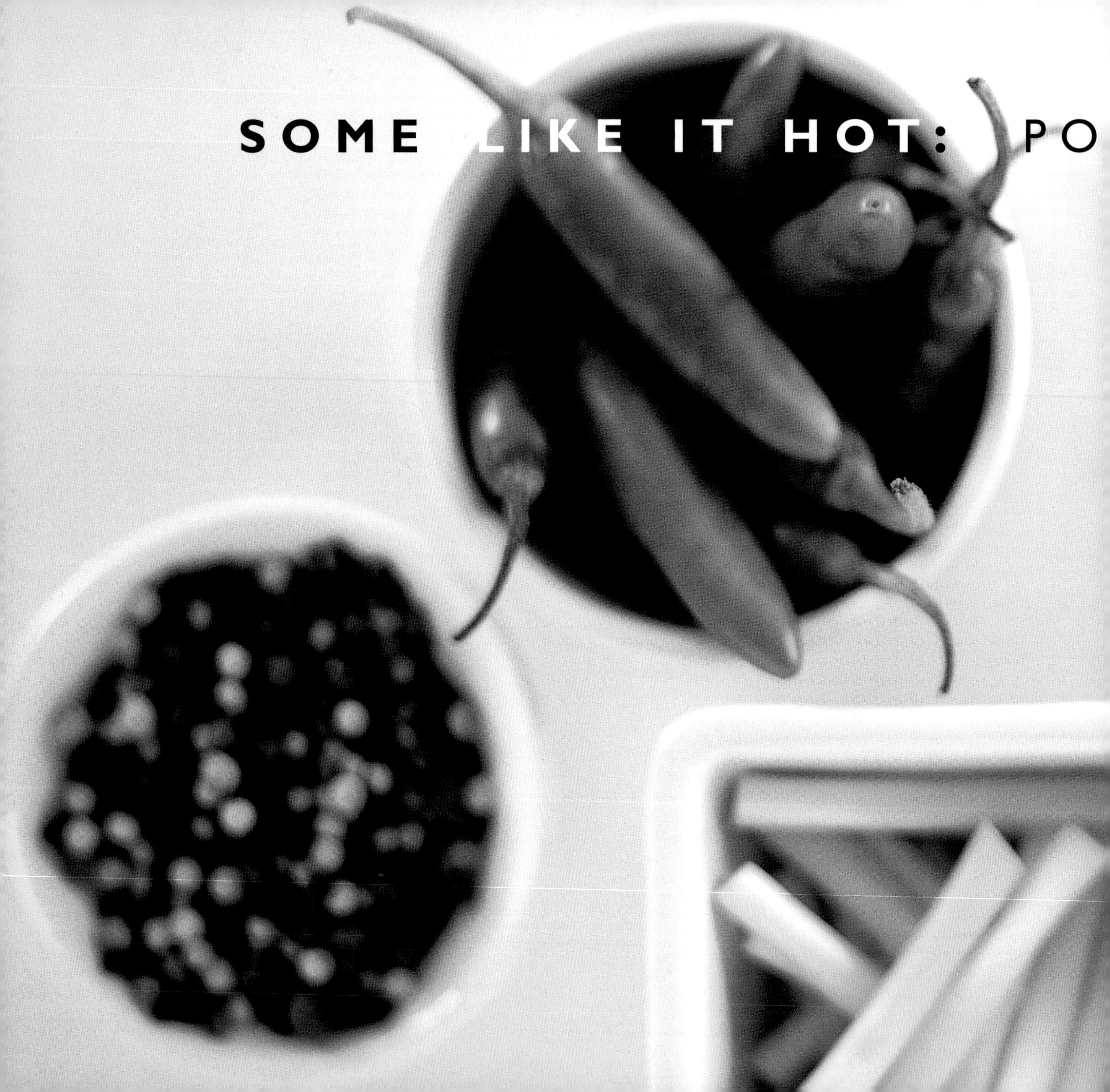

ATO SALAD "CASSEROLES"

Potatoes Night Out

BORN AND RAISED IN NEW HAMPSHIRE, TROY TORR IS A YOUNG, UP-AND-COMING CHEF WHO HAS TRAINED IN PRESTIGIOUS RESTAURANTS IN THE CARIBBEAN AND IN BOSTON. THIS IS HIS RECIPE, WHICH WORKS WELL AS A LUNCHEON SALAD DISH WHEN SERVED ON A BED OF MESCLUN (SALAD GREENS) OR AS A SALAD ACCOMPANIMENT TO GRILLED MEAT OR FISH. WHEN YOU WANT A MORE FORMAL WARM SALAD PRESENTATION, THIS STOPS THE SHOW.

SERVES 6

SAUCE

2 cups Zinfandel
½ cup balsamic vinegar
4 whole cloves
½ cinnamon stick

5 cups water
2 teaspoons salt, plus salt to taste
About 2 pounds Yukon Gold potatoes
4 tablespoons olive oil
2 shallots, chopped (about 2 tablespoons)
4 portobello mushrooms, stems removed
  and caps thinly sliced
4 or 5 cloves garlic, chopped
  (about 2 tablespoons)
Pinch of ground nutmeg
1 teaspoon dried rosemary, crumbled
Freshly ground pepper to taste
1 cup freshly grated Parmesan cheese

To make the sauce, in a saucepan, combine the wine, vinegar, cloves, and cinnamon stick and bring to a boil over high heat. Reduce the heat to a simmer and cook until the liquid is reduced to about ¼ cup. This will take 30 to 35 minutes. Remove from the heat and let cool. Reserve at room temperature until serving. (The sauce may be made 2 to 3 days ahead, covered, and refrigerated until needed. Reheat gently for 5 minutes over medium-low heat.)

Preheat the oven to 400°F.

In a saucepan, combine the water and the 2 teaspoons salt. Slice the potatoes into thin ovals and add them to the water immediately to prevent discoloration.

When all of the potatoes are in the pan, place the pan over high heat and bring to a boil. Boil the potatoes until just tender but not falling apart, 1 to 2 minutes, depending on the thickness of the slices.

Meanwhile, place 2 tablespoons of the olive oil in a large bowl. When the potatoes are ready, drain well, add to the bowl, and toss the potatoes with the oil. Arrange the potato slices on a baking sheet in a single layer and refrigerate to cool. This keeps the starch and flavor in the potato.

(Recipe continues on p. 84.)

(Potatoes Night Out continued)

In a sauté pan over medium-high heat, warm the remaining 2 tablespoons oil. When the oil is hot, add the shallots and sauté for 1 minute. Add the mushrooms and sauté until soft, about 5 minutes. Toward the end of the cooking time, add the garlic, nutmeg, rosemary, salt, and pepper. Remove from the heat and let cool.

Select a 9-by-12-inch baking dish. Spray the dish lightly with vegetable oil spray. Using 2 or 3 potato slices for each base, make 6 bases, overlapping the slices slightly. Sprinkle with a little of the Parmesan cheese, top with a layer of mushroom slices, and again top with a little Parmesan cheese. Repeat to make 2 more layers each of potatoes and mushrooms, sprinkling each with a little cheese. Top each tower with a single potato slice and sprinkle with the remaining Parmesan cheese. Season with salt (not too much, as the cheese is salty) and pepper.

Bake the potato towers until the cheese turns brown and becomes crisp, about 15 minutes. Remove from oven and, using a broad spatula, transfer each tower to a plate. Drizzle with the Zinfandel sauce and serve immediately.

Pass the Potatoes

SERVES 4 TO 6

20 to 24 tiny new potatoes
½ cup unsalted butter
2 tablespoons minced shallot
2 teaspoons minced garlic
2 tablespoons chopped fresh curly parsley
1 tablespoon chopped fresh thyme, or
  1 teaspoon dried thyme, crumbled
Salt and freshly ground pepper to taste

Cook the potatoes according to the Master Recipe (page 16) for boiling potatoes, then drain. (Since these potatoes are very small, be careful not to overcook them.)

In a saucepan just large enough to accommodate the potatoes snugly, melt the butter over medium heat. Add the shallot and sauté until soft, 2 to 3 minutes. Add the garlic, parsley, and thyme and sauté for 1 to 2 minutes. Add the potatoes and shake the pan to cover them with the butter-herb mixture. Season with salt.

Cover tightly and cook until tender, 15 to 20 minutes. Check the potatoes from time to time to make sure they are not sticking; if too much liquid evaporates, add 1 or 2 tablespoons water, re-cover the pan, and continue cooking.

Remove from the heat and season with pepper. Transfer the potatoes to a warmed serving dish. Serve at once.

Hot Potato and Bratwurst Salad

ALTHOUGH THIS IS NOT TECHNICALLY A SALAD, NO COLLECTION OF MY POTATO FAVORITES WOULD BE COMPLETE WITHOUT IT. WHILE LIVING IN GERMANY FOR FOUR YEARS, MY FAMILY AND I LOOKED FORWARD TO THIS HEARTY DISH ON COLD NIGHTS. IT IS IMPORTANT TO FIND GOOD-QUALITY BRATWURST OR WEISSWURST (WHITE BRATWURST) FOR THIS RECIPE, WHICH COMES FROM MIMI SHERATON'S EXCELLENT *THE GERMAN COOKBOOK*. IT WAS MY BIBLE DURING OUR STAY!

SERVES 4 TO 6

2 1/2 pounds all-purpose potatoes

Salt and freshly ground pepper to taste

6 tablespoons freshly grated
   Parmesan cheese

1/2 cup unsalted butter, cut into small bits,
   plus 3 to 4 tablespoons butter, melted

6 to 8 bratwursts or weisswursts,
   about 1 1/2 pounds total

Sweet mustard, preferably flavored
   with horseradish

2 to 3 tablespoons fine cracker crumbs

Preheat the oven to 450°F. Butter a 9-by-13-inch baking dish.

Have ready a bowl three-fourths full of water. Very thinly slice the potatoes, making the slices as uniform as possible. (If the potatoes are not the same thickness, some will be cooked while others will remain raw.) As the potatoes are sliced, add them to the water. Let stand for 5 minutes, then drain and pat dry on paper towels.

Arrange a single layer of the potato slices in the prepared baking dish. Sprinkle with salt, pepper, and some of the Parmesan cheese and dot with some of the butter. Repeat to create more layers, sprinkling each one with the seasonings and cheese and dotting with the butter. Season the final layer with salt and pepper and top with all but 2 tablespoons of the cheese and all the remaining butter bits. Place the potatoes in the oven and bake for 15 minutes.

Meanwhile, bring a saucepan filled with water to a gentle boil, add the sausages, and parboil for 5 minutes. Remove the sausages from the water and cut a lengthwise slit down the center of each one. Fill each gash with some mustard.

When the potatoes have baked for 15 minutes, remove from the oven and place the sausages on top of them. Brush the sausages with the melted butter and sprinkle them with the remaining 2 tablespoons cheese. Sprinkle the cracker crumbs over the sausages and the top potato layer.

Return the baking dish to the oven and continue to bake until the potatoes are soft when pierced with a knife and the sausages are nicely browned on top, about 20 minutes longer. Serve directly from the baking dish.

Dee Dee's Pennsylvania Dutch Hot Potato Salad | DEE DEE ALAIMO,

WHO HAS BEEN DAZZLING HER FAMILY AND FRIENDS WITH SPECTACULAR MEALS FOR YEARS, CREATED THIS RECIPE FOR A SIMPLE HOT POTATO SALAD. IT IS ONE OF HER MOST REQUESTED RECIPES, AND EVERYONE IS SURPRISED TO LEARN THAT DEE DEE, WHO HAS FOREVER BEEN COOKING FROM THE PAGES OF JULIA CHILD, CRAIG CLAIBORNE, AND *GOURMET*, HAS A RECIPE THAT MAKES USE—AND FABULOUS USE AT THAT—OF VELVEETA CHEESE. THIS RECIPE CAN BE MADE IN ADVANCE AND KEPT IN THE REFRIGERATOR, COVERED, FOR SEVERAL HOURS BEFORE IT IS BAKED.

SERVES 8

2 pounds Yukon Gold potatoes

1½ to 2 cups mayonnaise, homemade
(page 19) or high-quality purchased

1 tablespoon yellow mustard (optional)

1 sweet onion such as Vidalia or Maui,
finely chopped

1 small package (8 ounces) Velveeta
cheese, cut into ¼-inch cubes

Salt to taste

3 slices bacon, chopped, and/or ¼ cup
pimiento green olives, sliced

Cook the potatoes according to the Master Recipe (see page 16) for boiling potatoes. When cool enough to handle, peel and cut into ⅜-inch cubes.

Meanwhile, preheat the oven to 350°F.

In a large bowl, combine 1½ cups of the mayonnaise, the mustard (if using), and the onion, and stir until well combined. Add the potatoes and the cheese, and more mayonnaise as needed to coat the potatoes completely. Season with salt.

Transfer the mixture to an 8-by-11-inch baking dish, and top with the bacon pieces or sliced olives, or both.

Bake until piping hot and bubbling, 35 to 45 minutes. Serve hot or warm.

Nuremberg Potato Salad

ON NEARBY SQUAM LAKE, THE GOLDEN POND OF FILM FAME, STANDS A BEAUTIFUL AND HISTORIC INN CALLED THE MANOR ON GOLDEN POND. THE INNKEEPERS, BRIAN AND MARY ELLEN SHIELDS, ARE CONSUMMATE HOSTS, MAINTAINING HIGH STANDARDS IN A BEAUTIFUL SETTING. MARY ELLEN, WHOSE FAMILY, THE NEMEYERS, CAME FROM NUREMBERG, GERMANY, SHARED HER FAMILY RECIPE FOR GERMAN POTATO SALAD, WHICH CAN BE SERVED EITHER HOT OR COLD.

SERVES 6

2 pounds Red Bliss potatoes

DRESSING

¾ cup diced bacon (¼ pound)
¾ cup minced yellow onion
1½ teaspoons flour
4 teaspoons sugar
1 teaspoon salt
¼ teaspoon freshly ground pepper
¼ to ⅓ cup cider vinegar
½ cup water
¼ cup finely chopped fresh curly parsley
1 teaspoon celery seed

Cook the potatoes according to the Master Recipe (page 16) for boiling potatoes. When cool enough to handle, cut into ¼-inch-thick slices. Place in a bowl.

Meanwhile, make the dressing: In a small skillet over medium heat, fry the bacon until just crisp, 5 to 6 minutes. Add ½ cup of the onion and sauté until just tender but not brown, 2 to 3 minutes. Remove from the heat.

In a small bowl, stir together the flour, sugar, salt, and pepper. Stir in ¼ cup of the vinegar and the ½ cup water until smooth. Taste and add more vinegar if the mixture is not tart enough. Add the flour mixture to the bacon, then simmer over low heat, stirring, until slightly thickened, 4 to 5 minutes.

Pour the hot dressing over the potatoes and add the remaining ¼ cup onion, the parsley, and the celery seed. Toss the salad by pouring it from one bowl to another until the potatoes are well coated.

Serve the salad immediately, or let cool, cover, and refrigerate overnight, then serve cold.

Gammy's Hot Potato Salad

WHEN I WAS A CHILD, VISITS TO MY GRANDPARENTS' HOME OVERLOOKING PENOBSCOT BAY, IN BELFAST, MAINE, WERE ALWAYS A TREAT. MY GRANDFATHER WAS THE MAYOR OF BELFAST AT THE TIME, AND MY "GAMMY" WAS A COOK OF NOTE! THIS OLD-FASHIONED RECIPE FROM HER IS STILL GOOD ON A COLD WINTER'S NIGHT. I HAVE UPDATED IT EVER SO SLIGHTLY.

SERVES 4 TO 6

2 pounds red or brown all-purpose potatoes
1 jar red pimiento, drained and chopped
1 cup diced celery, including leaves
10 pimiento-stuffed olives, halved lengthwise
2 hard-boiled eggs, cut lengthwise into eighths
1/4 cup high-quality purchased Ranch-style
   salad dressing
Chopped fresh curly parsley for garnish

WHITE SAUCE

1 cup low-fat or whole milk
2 tablespoons unsalted butter
2 tablespoons flour
1 1/2 teaspoons salt
1/4 teaspoon freshly ground pepper

Cook the potatoes according to the Master Recipe (page 16) for steaming potatoes. When cool enough to handle, peel and cut into 1/4-inch cubes.

To make the white sauce, in a small saucepan over medium heat, warm the milk just until bubbles appear along the edges of the pan. In a medium-sized saucepan over medium heat, melt the butter just until bubbling. Add the flour and cook, stirring, to prevent browning, until the butter and the flour are well combined, about 3 minutes. Add the warm milk all at once, stirring as you do, then stir constantly with a whisk or a wooden spoon until the sauce begins to thicken. Continue cooking and stirring until the sauce is the consistency of heavy cream, about 5 minutes. Stir in the salt and pepper.

Add the cubed potatoes to the white sauce and heat gently to serving temperature. Add the pimiento, celery, olives, eggs, and ranch dressing and mix gently.

Transfer to a serving bowl and garnish with the parsley. Serve hot.

"No Pressure" French Potato Salad

IN THESE BUSY TIMES, THE PRESSURE COOKER HAS ENJOYED A WELL-DESERVED RENAISSANCE. ROBIN MCKENZIE, WHO WORKS FOR A SWISS COMPANY THAT MANUFACTURES AN EXCELLENT MODEL, SHARED THIS RECIPE WITH ME. IT SEEMS ROBIN AND I BOTH STUDIED AT LA VARENNE IN PARIS, BUT NEVER MET UNTIL I BEGAN RESEARCH FOR THIS BOOK. WE DISCOVERED WE'D STUDIED WITH THE SAME CHEFS, AND HAD HAD MANY SIMILAR LIFE EXERIENCES! IN THIS RECIPE, ROBIN COMBINES HER LOVE OF FRENCH FOOD WITH THE PRACTICALITY OF THE PRESSURE COOKER.

SERVES 4 TO 6

1½ cups dry white wine

2 pounds Yukon Gold potatoes, cut lengthwise into wedges 1½ inches wide

Salt and freshly ground pepper to taste

½ pound young, tender green beans, trimmed

6 thick slices bacon

3 scallions, including tender green tops, cut into ½-inch pieces

½ cup finely chopped fresh curly parsley or chives

VINAIGRETTE

2 tablespoons champagne vinegar or white wine vinegar

1 tablespoon Dijon mustard

6 tablespoons extra-virgin olive oil

Salt and freshly ground pepper to taste

Pour the wine into the bottom of a 4-quart or larger pressure cooker. Place the trivet in the cooker and add the cut-up potatoes, salt, and pepper. Cover and cook according to the manufacturer's instructions. They should take 4 to 6 minutes.

While the potatoes are cooking, prepare the beans and bacon. Have ready a bowl of ice water. Bring a saucepan three-fourths full of water to a boil. Add the beans, parboil for 5 minutes, and drain. Immediately plunge the beans into the ice water to set the color and halt the cooking.

In a skillet, fry the bacon over medium heat until crisp, 5 to 6 minutes. Transfer to paper towels to drain and crumble into small pieces.

When the potatoes are ready, uncover and toss gently with the hot wine remaining in the pressure cooker. Then drain, place in a bowl, add the scallions, and allow to cool slightly.

To make the vinaigrette, in a small bowl, stir together the vinegar and mustard. Gradually whisk in the olive oil until a thick emulsion forms. Season with salt and pepper.

Add the vinaigrette to the potatoes and toss gently. Using a wooden spoon (so that you don't break up the soft potatoes), mix in the beans and bacon. Top with the parsley or chives and serve at once.

Jansson's Temptation

THIS SWEDISH DISH MADE ITS WAY ACROSS SCANDINAVIA TO GERMANY, WHERE I FIRST ENJOYED IT AT A POTLUCK SUPPER GIVEN AT THE FRANKFURT INTERNATIONAL SCHOOL IN OBERURSEL. MANY NATIONALITIES WERE REPRESENTED IN THE STUDENT BODY, AND THE POTLUCKS FEATURED AN ASTOUNDING ASSORTMENT OF SALADS, HOT AND COLD, FROM AROUND THE WORLD. IF YOU ARE NOT AN ANCHOVY OR HERRING LOVER, PLEASE TURN THE PAGE, BUT IF YOU ARE A MEMBER OF THE BAND OF DEVOTEES OF WHAT MY SON CALLS "FURRY FISH," READ ON! THIS HOT SALAD CAN EASILY BE TRANSPORTED AND REHEATED IN A 350°F OVEN FOR 15 MINUTES. IT CAN ALSO BE MADE WITH MATJES HERRING SPRATS, FOUND IN TINS. WHO JANSSON WAS IS LOST IN THE NORDIC MISTS. BUT WE'RE GLAD HE WAS TEMPTED.

SERVES 6 TO 8

2 pounds Yukon Gold potatoes

3 yellow onions, thinly sliced

2 tins (2 ounces each) anchovy fillets in olive oil, drained and oil reserved

1/4 to 1/3 cup unsalted butter, cut into small bits

Freshly ground pepper to taste

1/4 cup fresh bread crumbs

1 cup half-and-half or heavy cream

Preheat the oven to 375°F. Generously butter a 9-by-12-inch rectangular or oval baking dish. Have ready a large bowl three-fourths full of cold water.

Peel the potatoes, slipping them into the water as they are peeled to prevent discoloration. Remove them from the water and cut into strips as you would for French fries, then return the strips to the water until ready to cook.

Cut the onions in half horizontally. Place flat-side down on a cutting board and thinly slice vertically.

Drain and blot the potatoes dry. Cut the anchovy fillets into small pieces. Cover the base of the baking dish with a thin layer of potatoes and then one of onions. Top with some of the small anchovy pieces. Scatter bits of the butter among the pieces of fish and sprinkle lightly with pepper. Continue alternating layers of the potatoes, onions, anchovies, and butter, sprinkling each layer with pepper, until all the potatoes, onions, and anchovies are used up and ending with a layer of potatoes. Reserve some of the butter for the top. Sprinkle the bread crumbs evenly over the top and dot generously with the remaining butter. Sprinkle with the reserved anchovy oil.

Bake the dish for 20 minutes. Remove from the oven and pour half of the cream very carefully down one side so that you don't disturb the bread crumbs. Return the dish to the oven and bake for 10 minutes longer. Again, remove the dish from the oven and add the remaining cream in the same way. Return the dish to the oven and bake until the contents are bubbling and the potatoes are tender when pierced with a knife, 15 to 20 minutes longer.

Remove from the oven and let rest for 5 to 10 minutes. Serve warm.

Church Supper Potluck Hot Ham and Potato Salad | OUR CHURCH

IN MEREDITH, NEW HAMPSHIRE, IS THE SCENE OF MANY WONDERFUL POTLUCK SUPPERS. WHETHER IT IS THE WEDNESDAY-NIGHT CHRISTIAN EDUCATION PROGRAM OR THE CHURCH'S ANNUAL MEETING, NOTHING BRINGS THE CONGREGATION OF TRINITY CHURCH TOGETHER MORE QUICKLY THAN POTLUCK. NO MATTER HOW MANY PEOPLE SHOW UP, A GREAT VARIETY IS ALWAYS AVAILABLE, AND LIKE IN THE STORY OF THE LOAVES AND FISHES, THERE IS PLENTY OF FOOD FOR ALL. THIS SALAD TRAVELS WELL AND CAN BE EITHER REHEATED OR SERVED AT ROOM TEMPERATURE WHEN IT REACHES ITS DESTINATION.

SERVES 8 TO 10

1 ½ pounds Yukon Gold potatoes

½ pound boiled or baked ham, in one piece, cut into ½-inch cubes

1 cup shredded sharp Cheddar cheese

1 cup sour cream, full fat or low fat

½ cup mayonnaise, homemade (page 19) or high-quality purchased

1 tablespoon Dijon mustard

2 large eggs, beaten

3 tablespoons sliced scallions, white part only, tender green parts reserved

1 teaspoon salt

½ teaspoon freshly ground pepper

Dash of Tabasco or other hot-pepper sauce

¼ cup freshly grated Parmesan cheese

Preheat the oven to 350°F. Butter a shallow 9-by-11-inch baking dish.

Cook the potatoes according to the Master Recipe (page 16) for boiling potatoes. When cool enough to handle, peel and cut into ½-inch cubes. Combine the potatoes and ham in the prepared baking dish.

In a bowl, stir together the Cheddar cheese, sour cream, mayonnaise, mustard, eggs, sliced white scallions, salt, pepper, and hot-pepper sauce until well combined. Pour the mixture evenly over the potatoes and ham. Sprinkle the surface evenly with the Parmesan cheese.

Bake until set, about 30 minutes. Remove from the oven. Thinly slice the reserved green scallion tops and scatter over the top. Serve immediately or at room temperature.

THE CELEBRITIES: A CO

Deborah Madison—Potato Salad with Tomatillo Sauce

DEBORAH MADISON'S BOOKS LIFT VEGETARIAN COOKING TO A NEW LEVEL. SHE IS THE AUTHOR OF SEVERAL EXCELLENT BOOKS ON THE SUBJECT, WITH MANY OF THE RECIPES GLEANED FROM HER DAYS AS CHEF AT GREENS, A NOTED SAN FRANCISCO RESTAURANT. THIS UNUSUAL POTATO SALAD, FROM *THE SAVORY WAY*, IS A FEAST FOR THE EYES AS WELL AS THE TASTE BUDS. MADISON SUGGESTS THAT IF YOU USE THE OPTIONAL OIL, DRESS THE SALAD JUST BEFORE SERVING. IF YOU'D LIKE A HOTTER SAUCE, RESERVE HALF THE GARLIC AND HALF THE JALAPEÑOS AND ADD THEM UNCOOKED TO THE TOMATILLOS AS THEY'RE BEING PURÉED. FOR A CREAMIER SAUCE, ADD ¼ CUP SOUR CREAM OR PLAIN YOGURT.

SERVES 4 TO 6

1½ pounds red-skinned or yellow-fleshed new potatoes

6 plump tomatillos, husks removed (see note)

1 or 2 jalapeño chiles, halved lengthwise and seeded

½ yellow onion, cut into several pieces

3 cloves garlic

1 cup fresh cilantro leaves, plus sprigs for garnish

1 to 2 tablespoons peanut, sunflower, or other light oil (optional)

Grated zest and juice of 1 lime

Salt to taste

2 hard-boiled eggs, sliced

6 radishes

If the skins on the potatoes look fresh, leave them on. Otherwise, peel the potatoes and cut them into ¼-inch-thick slices. Cook according to the Master Recipe (page 16) for steaming potatoes. Steam until tender but still firm, about 15 minutes. Remove the potatoes from the steamer and let them cool.

While the potatoes are steaming, make the sauce: Fill a saucepan with water and bring to a boil. Add the tomatillos, jalapeño(s), onion, and garlic, reduce the heat to medium, and simmer until the tomatillos turn from a bright to a dull green, 10 to 15 minutes. Drain, transfer to a food processor or a blender, add the cilantro leaves, and purée until smooth. Stir in the oil, if using, and the lime zest and juice. Season with salt.

Arrange the cooled potatoes on a platter or in a shallow bowl. Intersperse the egg slices among the potato slices. Ladle the tomatillo sauce over all. Garnish with the radishes and cilantro sprigs and serve.

NOTE 3 medium-sized green tomatoes may be substituted for tomatillos.

Giuliano Bugialli—Potato Salad, Florentine Style | GIULIANO BUGIALLI

TEACHES COOKING ON BOTH SIDES OF THE ATLANTIC. HE HAS MANY EXCELLENT BOOKS TO HIS CREDIT AND A LEGION OF DEVOTED STUDENTS, MYSELF INCLUDED. MY TIME IN HIS CLASSES IN FLORENCE WAS A HIGHLIGHT OF MY CULINARY EDUCATION. HE IS A TRUE CLASSICIST IN HIS APPROACH TO COOKING, THE INTEGRITY OF THE INGREDIENTS BEING THE MOST IMPORTANT ELEMENT. THIS RECIPE IS FROM *THE FINE ART OF ITALIAN COOKING*, BUGIALLI'S FIRST BOOK. HE SUGGESTS SERVING IT WITH LIGHTLY FLAVORED MAIN DISHES AND FOR BUFFETS.

SERVES 4 TO 6

Coarse sea salt or kosher salt

2 pounds all-purpose brown-
 skinned potatoes

4 salt-packed anchovies or
 8 olive-oil anchovy fillets

¼ cup olive oil

Freshly ground pepper to taste

1 tablespoon fresh flat-leaf parsley leaves

Fill a large saucepan or stockpot three-fourths full of water and add salt. Bring to a boil and add the potatoes. Cook until tender but still firm, 25 to 30 minutes. Drain and place the potatoes on a cutting board. When cool enough to handle, peel them, then let cool to room temperature, about 25 minutes.

Meanwhile, ready the anchovies. If using salt-packed anchovies, fillet them and rinse under cold running water, draining well. If using fillets in oil, drain. Coarsely chop the anchovies.

Cut the potatoes into 1-inch cubes and place in a serving bowl. Add the anchovies, olive oil, and pepper. Mix all the ingredients together gently but thoroughly. Sprinkle the parsley leaves over the top and serve.

Marcella Hazan—Potato Salad Marcella

WHILE LIVING IN EUROPE, I WAS FORTUNATE ENOUGH TO TAKE CLASSES FROM CELEBRATED AUTHOR AND TEACHER MARCELLA HAZAN IN BOLOGNA, ITALY. ABOVE ALL, SHE STRESSED FRESHNESS AND SIMPLICITY, TWO PARAMOUNT CHARACTERISTICS OF ITALIAN CUISINE. THIS IS HER RECIPE FOR POTATO SALAD, FROM HER INDISPENSABLE *ESSENTIALS OF ITALIAN COOKING*, A COMPENDIUM OF HER FIRST AND SECOND BOOKS. YUKON GOLD POTATOES WORK WELL IN THIS SALAD. ALL OF THE INGREDIENTS MUST BE OF THE HIGHEST QUALITY.

SERVES 4 TO 6

1½ pounds medium-starch potatoes, either new or mature and of uniform size, or Yukon Gold potatoes

Red wine vinegar

Salt

Extra-virgin olive oil

Place the potatoes in a saucepan with water to cover by at least 2 inches. Bring slowly to a boil and cook gently until tender but not too soft, about 35 minutes, or less if you are using small new potatoes. Refrain from prodding them too frequently with the fork, or they will become soggy or break apart later when slicing them.

When done, pour off all the water from the pan, but leave the potatoes in it. Shake the pan over medium heat for just a few moments, moving the potatoes around, to evaporate all the excess moisture.

Transfer the potatoes to a cutting board and pull off the skins while they are still hot. Using a sharp knife and very little pressure, cut the potatoes into slices about ¼ inch thick. Spread them out on a warmed serving platter. Sprinkle immediately with about 3 tablespoons of vinegar and turn the potatoes gently.

When ready to serve, add salt and a liberal quantity of very good olive oil. Taste and correct for seasoning, adding more vinegar if required. Serve while still lukewarm or no colder than room temperature. Do not keep overnight, and do not refrigerate.

Jacques Pépin—Lentil and Potato Salad

JACQUES PÉPIN IS ONE OF THE FINEST COOKING TEACHERS I KNOW. AS WELL AS BEING AN EXTRAORDINARY CHEF AND TELEVISION PERSONALITY, PÉPIN LENDS HIS TIME AND TALENT TO THE INTERNATIONAL ASSOCIATION OF COOKING PROFESSIONALS, WHICH ASSISTS MANY ASPIRING CULINARY ARTISTS WITH THEIR EDUCATION THROUGH A SCHOLARSHIP PROGRAM. IN THIS RECIPE, JACQUES USES THE TINY GREEN FRENCH LENTILS, *LENTILLES DU PUY*, BECAUSE THEY HOLD THEIR SHAPE WELL AS THEY COOK. IF THEY ARE NOT AVAILABLE, YOU MAY SUBSTITUTE ANY OTHER DRIED LENTIL. JACQUES SUGGESTS SERVING THE SALAD WITH SLICES OF A GOOD SAUSAGE ARRANGED ON TOP.

SERVES 4

¾ cup dried lentils (about 4½ ounces), preferably lentilles du Puy

1 teaspoon salt

2¾ cups water

4 small to medium-sized brown all-purpose potatoes, about ¾ pound total

¾ cup finely chopped yellow onion

3 or 4 cloves garlic, crushed and then finely chopped (2 teaspoons)

¼ cup chopped fresh herb mixture, consisting of equal parts parsley, basil, savory, and tarragon

3 or 4 scallions, including tender green tops, finely minced (3 tablespoons)

¼ cup virgin olive oil

2 tablespoons red wine vinegar

½ teaspoon freshly ground pepper

In a large saucepan, combine the lentils, ¼ teaspoon of the salt, and the water. Bring to a boil, cover, adjust the heat so that the water boils gently, and cook until the lentils are tender, about 45 minutes. Remove the pan from the heat and let the lentils cool, covered, for 15 minutes in the liquid. (Most of the liquid should have been absorbed.)

Meanwhile, place the potatoes in a saucepan with cold water to cover. Bring to a boil over high heat, reduce the heat to low, and cook the potatoes gently, uncovered, until tender when pierced with the tip of a knife, about 35 minutes, adding water as needed to keep the potatoes covered. Drain and when cool enough to handle, cut crosswise into ⅜-inch-thick slices and place in a bowl.

Add the lentils to the potatoes and stir gently to combine. Add the yellow onion, garlic, herbs, scallions, olive oil, vinegar, pepper, and the remaining ¾ teaspoon salt and mix just enough to combine well.

Transfer the salad to a large platter. Serve immediately while still warm.

ACKNOWLEDGMENTS

My deepest thanks and gratitude go to:

CH, my son, and his wife, Lisa; and my daughter, Lisa Laskin, and her husband, Bill; for their encouragement, listening, and testing.

My sister, Jo, and her husband, Tom, and Carlie and Greg for their support and contributions.

Lydia Torr and her staff at the Meredith, New Hampshire Public Library, and the Friday walking group for all their taste-testing.

Judy Rich, for her culinary contribution and Yankee common sense.

Liz Lapham, my friend and colleague, who came through snow and ice to edit, test, and taste, and, above all else, to encourage me with her unfailing good humor.

Susan Ginsburg, my literary agent, for her encouragement and support.

Bill LeBlond, my editor at Chronicle Books, for having faith in my book.

Amy Treadwell, also at Chronicle Books, for her guidance and enormous patience in taking me through the editorial process gently and with kindness.

Sharon Silva, my copy editor, for her sense of detail.

Jan Hughes, at Chronicle Books, for her incredible ability for fine-tuning.

Tom Wilson, for all of the above reasons, and just for being there.

A

Alaimo, Dee Dee, 88

All-purpose potatoes (red or brown), 12, 13
  Alpine Potato and Cheese Salad, 66
  Blue-Ribbon Southern Potato Salad, 22
  Gammy's Hot Potato Salad, 91
  Hot Potato and Bratwurst Salad, 87
  Lentil and Potato Salad, 102
  Marie's French Potato Salad, 73
  Marsh Family Mashed Potato Salad, 23
  Potato Salad, Florentine Style, 100
  Potato Salad for a Crowd, 43
  Roasted Garlic Potato Salad, 27
  Rosemary-Orange Potato Salad, 29
  "Stop and Go" Italian Potato Salad, 72

Alpine Potato and Cheese Salad, 66

Anchovies
  Jansson's Temptation, 94
  Niçoise Potato Salad, 75
  Potato Salad, Florentine Style, 100

Artichoke hearts
  Crabmeat and Potato Salad, 57
  Red Pesto Potato Salad, 30, 32

B

Bacon
  Dee Dee's Pennsylvania Dutch Hot Potato Salad, 88
  "No Pressure" French Potato Salad, 92
  Nuremberg Potato Salad, 90

Basil. See Pesto

Beans
  New Year's Day Good Luck Salad, 35
  Niçoise Potato Salad, 75
  "No Pressure" French Potato Salad, 92
  Pesto Potato Salad, 70
  Portuguese Potato Salad, 76

Beef
  Irish Potato Salad, An, 67
  Steak and Potatoes Salad, 45

Blue-Ribbon Southern Potato Salad, 22

Broccoli
  Frog Potato Salad, The, 40

Brody, Lora, 44

Bugialli, Giuliano, 100

C

Cauliflower
  Camp Island Potato Salad, 25

Cheese
  Alpine Potato and Cheese Salad, 66
  Church Supper Potluck Hot Ham and Potato Salad, 95
  Dee Dee's Pennsylvania Dutch Hot Potato Salad, 88
  Greek Potato Salad, 69
  Potatoes Night Out, 83–84
  Steak and Potatoes Salad, 45
  "Stop and Go" Italian Potato Salad, 72

Chef Woolley's Grilled Potato Salad, 38

Church Supper Potluck Hot Ham and Potato Salad, 95

Crabmeat and Potato Salad, 57

Curried Potato Salad, 78

D

Dee Dee's Pennsylvania Dutch Hot Potato Salad, 88

Denny's Boiled Dressing, 67

F

Fabulous Fourth Salmon and Potato Salad, 53

Fennel
  Potato Salad Molly Malone, 63

Fiddlehead ferns
  New England Spring Potato Salad, 24

Fingerling potatoes, 12
  Moulton Farm Potato Salad, 37
  Smoked Trout and Potato Salad, 56

Fish. *See also* Anchovies
  Fabulous Fourth Salmon and Potato Salad, 53
  Niçoise Potato Salad, 75
  Smoked Trout and Potato Salad, 56
  Sunday Morning Smoked Salmon Potato Salad, 58

French Dressing, 43

Frog Potato Salad, The, 40

G

Gammy's Hot Potato Salad, 91

Garlic Potato Salad, Roasted, 27

Graham, Robby, 56, 57, 58

Greek Potato Salad, 69

H

Ham
  Church Supper Potluck Hot Ham and Potato Salad, 95
  New Hampshire Mapled Ham and Potato Salad, 50

Hazan, Marcella, 101

Herbst, Sharon Tyler, 48

Home-Run Potato Salad, 44

Horseradish Potato Salad, 42

Hot dogs
  Home-Run Potato Salad, 44
  Hot Potato and Bratwurst Salad, 87

I

Irish Potato Salad, An, 67

J

Jansson's Temptation, 94

Jo's Asian Potato Salad, 64

K

Kennebec potatoes, 13

L

Lamb Potato Salad, Tarragon, 47

Lapham, Liz and Bev, 25

La Rouge potatoes, 13

La Soda potatoes, 13

Leak, Anna, 22

Lentil and Potato Salad, 102

Lobster Roll Potato Salad, 54

Long White potatoes, 13

M

Madison, Deborah, 98

Maple syrup, 50

Marie's French Potato Salad, 73

Marsh Family Mashed Potato Salad, 23

Mayonnaise, 19

McKenzie, Robin, 92

Moulton Farm Potato Salad, 37

Mushrooms
  Potatoes Night Out, 83–84

Mussels
  Potato Salad Molly Malone, 63

N

New England Mustard-Pickle Potato Salad, 26

New England Spring Potato Salad, 24

New Hampshire Mapled Ham and Potato Salad, 50

New potatoes, 12. *See also* Red new potatoes
  Jo's Asian Potato Salad, 64
  Pass the Potatoes, 85
  Potato Salad Marcella, 101
  Potato Salad with Tomatillo Sauce, 98

New Year's Day Good Luck Salad, 35

Niçoise Potato Salad, 75

"No Pressure" French Potato Salad, 92

Nuremberg Potato Salad, 90

Nuts, toasting, 17

O

Onions, 13

Orange Potato Salad, Rosemary, 29

Oyster Potato Salad, Smoked, 51

P

Pass the Potatoes, 85

Pasta
  Pesto Potato Salad, 70